Life Rolls on;The journey frc

By

Tony Trevor Baker

Dedicated to my mother

Who never got to see her son grow up and see the man I became.

Copyright©2012.

Published by Lulu.com

www.liferollson.co.uk

Cover design by Russell Gardner.

ISBN no 9781471752100

Contents

Prologue. P5

Part 1; Rolling downhill.

Chapter 1; *The day that everything changed.* **P7**

Chapter 2; *The injury.* **P13**

Chapter 3; *The first three months.* **P18**

Chapter 4; *Getting up and mobile.* **P26**

Chapter 5; *Nursing home.* **P34**

Part 2; Rolling forward.

Chapter 6; *Home.* **P39**

Chapter 7; *Wheels and transport.* **P48**

Chapter 8; *Hiring and firing.* **P54**

Chapter 9; *Reiki and spirituality.* **P57**

Chapter 10; *Music and live entertainment.* **P60**

Chapter 11; *Walk a mile in my shoes.* **P64**

Part 3; Rolling around the world.

Chapter 12; *Back up Skiing.* **P84**

Chapter 13; *Back up Multi activity.* **P93**

Chapter 14; *Egypt.* **P100**

Chapter 15; *Holidays.* **P107**

Chapter 16; *Norfolk.* **P112**

Chapter 17; *Free as a bird.* **P115**

Part 4; Rolling backwards.

Chapter 18; *Mishaps.* **P118**

Chapter 19: *Chair problems.* **P126**

Chapter 20: *People's attitude towards disability.* **P130**

Part 5; Rolling back time.

Chapter 21; *Skating.* **P136**

Chapter 22; *Snow.* **P144**

Chapter 23; *Bikes.* **P155**

Chapter 24; *Reflections and the impact of losing my mother.* **P163**

Chapter 25; *Fundown at Sundown.* **P169**

Chapter 26: *Work.* **P174**

Chapter 27; *Tattoos.* **P182**

Part 6; Rolling up towards a degree.

Chapter 28; *Starting college.* **P189**

Chapter 29; *Boccia.* **P197**

Chapter 30; *The SAND club.* **P200**

Chapter 31; *Sport relief mile 2012.* **P208**

Chapter 32; *Inclusive sports project.* **P211**

Chapter 33; *Teacher training.* **P214**

Chapter 34; *Counselling at college.* **P216**

Chapter 35; *Counselling at university.* **P222**

Prologue

Hello and thank you for purchasing my book. My name is Tony Trevor Baker (B.A) although I prefer to be called Trev or T. At time of writing I am 37 years old.

I have written this book to get my life story out there and my hope is that my narrative can help people understand more about living with paralysis or any disability of which there are many. To create more awareness of what can be experienced or achieved whilst dealing with adversity. I hope my experiences can help people with disabilities or family members and friends or people that are able bodied adapt to whatever life has thrown at you. I also hope it will help people understand the need to look past a wheelchair and see the person in it for who they are.

I hope people will read this and it will inspire / push you into taking that leap of faith you have always been dreaming of, whether it's going skiing, enjoying sailing, quad biking, pushing your limits, moving house, seeing the great pyramids, gaining a degree or learning a new skill. All of which were my hopes and fears that I have reached after breaking my neck and being told I would never walk again. I explain how practical issues have been resolved, like buying a power chair and a vehicle. I also talk about some of my memories before my accident.

This is my story about my journey from being able bodied (AB) to gaining a degree and becoming a Bachelor of Arts (BA).I hope that you enjoy reading it and take something away from it.

Please feel free to email me any comments or feedback or questions that have arisen and I will try to answer to the best of my knowledge or point you in the right direction.

liferollsonbook@gmail.com

Enjoy.

Part 1; Rolling down hill

Chapter 1

The day that everything changed

In order to celebrate the millennium myself aged 25 and friends had arranged to go to Edinburgh to celebrate the New Year.

We went up a couple of days prior to the New Year and had a couple of drinking nights in the city.

On the morning of New Year's Eve we went into a coffee bar, I remember needing caffeine others may have had alcohol but I certainly didn't.

We were walking around the city trying to pass time, and came across a tour for the underground of Edinburgh.

Edinburgh is renowned for its history and paranormal activity.

We went into the tour and the first thing we saw was a room clearly locked which looked as though modern day witchcraft went on.

As the tour progressed we were told various ghost stories etc, some of which were very convincing.

I do remember one story where the guy said five or six people in a particular group all fell forward at the same time, all of them said it felt like they had been pushed from behind but there was no one there.

We went to one particular room where there was a stone circle. Most people instinctively stood outside, I went into the middle and the guy said I was stood directly where the energies enter and exit the circle, I thought that was typical.

After we had left the underground caverns I said to my friends I had a really strange feeling in my spine they all made fun of me saying how scared I was whilst underground.

I didn't really give it much thought until afterwards.

I have always felt it was a premonition my life was going to change and some force made my life change.

We went for a pint, and then decided to find a high point to get a good view of the city.

We came across Arthur's seat which is near the castle, it is a large mound; on one edge was a rocky face.

My mate decided to climb it and for some reason I followed, the rest of the group took the sensible route and followed the path. I wasn't a climber and had no safety equipment on which was out of character for me.

It was wet and slippery.

At some point I lost my gripping and fell and broke my neck during the fall, I was conscious at the bottom and initially thought I would die, having broken many bones in my body as I couldn't move.

I remember being conscious and with it enough to be able to tell the paramedics I am allergic to penicillin.

My friend made it to the top after seeing me fall, he thought I was dead. He got to the top regrouped with everyone and said what had happened to me, luckily and thankfully other people saw the accident and called Mountain rescue.

By the time everyone else had gotten back down the paramedics were there.

At some point I thought I heard my mother's voice saying 'not yet'. My mother died in 93.

I do believe I will see her again and this was either a drug induced fantasy or a connection with the afterlife, where she was saying it is not my time yet.

I was taken to Edinburgh Infirmary about an hour or so after having a strange feeling in the underground with suspected spinal cord injury.

My father and partner found out quite quickly and came up to Edinburgh. They must have had discussions with doctors and wanted to get me as near home as possible and under the care of the right consultants so I was flown down to Sheffield spinal injury unit New Year's Day.

My brother and friends were at a party in my old flat as one house mate stayed at home. I can only imagine the devastation of how everyone close to me found out.

X-rays were taken in Edinburgh which I found horrible to see, seeing the actual damage but thankfully they didn't operate and butcher my neck.

The doctors in Edinburgh decided not to operate and get me to specialists who decided to put me on traction for three months with the intention of healing more naturally.

In that one moment that one slip, that one error it was the most expensive mistake I have ever made it nearly cost me my life and changed everything I knew about life.

Chapter 2

The injury

I broke my neck at Legion C4, which is four vertebras' from the skull, and damaged a lower vertebra in my back roughly about where I had a strange feeling.

There was no internal damage to any organs.

The technical term for my disability is tetraplegia, although in America the term is quadriplegic i.e. damage or paralysis to 4 limbs, people that break their backs or lower down the spine are known as paraplegic i.e. half the body is paralysed below the point of injury.

The spinal column starts at C1 where the skull attaches to the spine. This is known as a hangman's break, Christopher Reeves broke his neck here.

The vertebras' job is to offer flexibility in the body and protect the spinal cord; the spinal cord is what delivers messages from the brain to the body in order for it to function.C1-C3 allow the head and neck to move, C4 operates the diaphragm, C5 makes the deltoids or shoulders move and is also responsible for controlling biceps. C5-C7 operate triceps wrists and hands.

The thoracic section operates the back and the core.

The lower part of vertebrae operates leg muscles.

There are 2 types of spinal cord injury known as a complete injury when a person has little or no feeling or sensation below the point of injury, and then there is incomplete injury damage to the spinal cord and sensation is felt below the point of injury.

Mine was an incomplete injury whereas I heavily bruised the spinal cord meaning that messages do get through, from the brain and body but are misinterpreted and the motor neurons that control muscle movement do not work very well.

Due to being an incomplete injury I've always had pretty good sensation and very limited movement, I've always been able to move various bits just not enough for any kind of function for example I can move my toes.

Due to having a high level injury I breathe purely from the diaphragm and when I lay down flat my chest doesn't expand, which was always a worry in regards to chest infections.

Bladder and bowel function are usually the first to go in spinal injury, luckily my bladder was still working and emptying as normal, lots of people have to do regular catheters every two or three hours to manually empty the bladder. I have to wear a convene which goes directly into a leg bag which is much more hygienic and much less hassle and discomfort.

There was always concern with spinal injury about skin breaking down and pressure sores occurring, I have been very lucky regarding this.

One of the major issues regarding spinal injury is autonomic dysflexia, as the spinal cord operates the nervous system, this occurs when there is something physically wrong in my body this can range from anything from internal damage, having an ingrown toe nail, overheating, bladder or bowels being blocked or anything which is wrong that the body can't feel below the lower level of injury.

I'm very lucky and have good sensation throughout and usually know if something is wrong.

I have been autonomic a few times early on; it can be fatal although I used to carry a spray around just in case which will be sprayed onto the tongue which brings the pressure down.

I get dizzy and light-headed and very clammy and my heart starts beating very fast, usually the spray brought me around although district nurses had to be called out a couple of times.

The worst time was the second time I went to Sweden and used a catheter, before boarding the plane we went to empty the leg bag, and it was full of blood. Luckily there were nurses around; the balloon inside the bladder had become dislodged.

I was nearly passing out on the plane, when we landed it was sorted out properly and taken out and I haven't used one since, I don't recommend having a pipe inserted into your manhood.

In hospital there always seemed to be someone going autonomic and it was quite scary to watch.

Chapter 3

The first three months

The first three months of 2000 were spent completely flat on my back with weights attached to the back of the head, and unable to move at all.

This involved having my skull drilled into the sides and I had a halo just above my forehead, thankfully out of sight but the weights hung to the back of a halo and every few weeks or so the weight was increased. It was like having my head stuck in a vice.

Initially I thought I had also suffered some brain damage as I had hallucinations of the hospital being built around me and the noise was intense I kept seeing and smelling oranges of some description, this is a vague memory but I do recall driving the nurses mental with some kind of orange obsession, and I am not really sure what that was all about, initially it was probably morphine.

I had a mirror above my bed and always had to look into that whenever talking to someone as I couldn't move my head. I had to eat on my back which was extremely difficult so I had supplements to survive.

I lost the majority of muscle mass. Doctors were constantly doing sensation tests with a pin, seeing where sensation was.

I was told the severity of the break straight away, although was on the effects of morphine and in denial for a couple of weeks.

One of the first things I remember the doctor saying was that there was a very good chance of survival and a very good chance I'll never walk again.

There was no way to process this information I would just dwell on it for a long time and I tried to focus more on the staying alive part.

I was in a room with three other people who were still in acute stages of spinal injury, so there was always conversation no matter what time of day it was although everyone was in similar situations.

I don't recall talking much about how I was unless it was family. I did talk to a lot of patients as they were going up similar creeks without paddles.

Nurses would try to be empathetic, saying; I know how you feel! This would really irritate me as although they have probably seen hundreds of cases they were able to get up and walk and look after themselves, which always made me jealous.

I became good friends with the man in the next bed and it was about three months before we spoke face-to-face and I was able to put a face to the voice.

During this period all I could do was think about everything I had lost, there wasn't any point looking forward to what the future may hold it was purely survival day-to-day.

I would see the doctors every week and they would monitor how traction was helping to heal my neck.

It was always a relief when family or friends visited although there wasn't really anything they could do other than being there.

I was very surprised how quickly they let me drink alcohol in moderation, I think looking back doctors and nurses realised it helped numb the pain and was the only real pleasure available.

There were occasions when friends and my brother would move me on the bed and get me stoned which wouldn't take much, most of the time I ended up passing out which didn't go down too well with the nurses, so I decided it probably wasn't the best idea. I found it would always be great being able to laugh again.

There were TVs on the walls so daytime TV helped pass the time, if there was something specific I wanted to watch it had to be agreed with the others in advance. Most of the time no one cared what was on the telly it was just noise and distraction.

It was during this time whilst on traction and bed rest my friend who climbed with me wrote an emotional heart touching song called Sleepwalkers.

There are five stages of the grieving process. The first stage is denial and isolation, the second is anger, the third is bargaining, then fourth is depression and the final stage is acceptance.

These aren't necessarily just for bereavement they can be applied to loss in general.

When I accepted my reality and came out of denial, I was so angry at myself for being so stupid, so angry at my mum for not protecting me, although now I feel the reason I am still alive is because she was protecting me.

I was angry for living and didn't really want to.

I had spent three months entirely on a bed, unable to do anything for myself, toileting, eating, dressing, nothing to do except lay there. Depression kicked in and I had no will to live.

I'm not religious but I did pray and bargain for some kind of life back.

I was unable to do anything for myself and had to learn to trust others with my care.

It is amazing as human beings how much is taken for granted, and when I could not do basic tasks for myself, I questioned my purpose.

After 8 months I left hospital and went into a nursing home for a further 4 months, my depression hit rock bottom, being surrounded by disabled people.

I thought what have I become, what do I do now?

Being surrounded by people who were worse off than me was strange, in a sense I was getting better and some were dying.

Waiting in the nursing home seemed to take for ever I knew I had a skiing holiday to look forward to and that was probably the only thing keeping me going and within just over a year of having my accident, I was in Sweden hurtling down a mountain in an adapted ski kart (more on that later).

It was at this moment I had clarity of acceptance, and thought: If I can ski, and still enjoy the excitement, the adrenaline, the thrill, the at-oneness, then perhaps all is not lost and I can still enjoy my life.

For me it was important although not obvious at the time to grieve for my old self.

The realisation of going through the mourning process for all that I had lost was a way of finding the strength of my inner Indestructible world.

Chapter 4

Getting up and mobile

I was ecstatic after three months that my neck had healed enough I would be finally able to get off the bed and put clothes on, even if they were jogging bottoms and be able to see the surroundings and start physiotherapy and occupational therapy, and get some fresh air.

I had to wear a neck brace for the first month or so to help take the weight.

I was so keen to get up and about although it wasn't an easy process.

Due to being just laid flat for such a long period I had to have my back slowly raised up a few degrees at a time, after about an hour I was sat at about 45° and was finally able to sit in a wheelchair.

This I only managed for about half an hour before getting too dizzy and light headed but it was amazing to be able to see people's faces when talking to them, and feel fresh air again and be able to have a quick look around the actual hospital and facilities where I'd been for three months with no idea what was outside the ward.

After a few days going through this rigmarole I was able to start therapy.

Initially this involved getting back on a physiotherapy bed, how ironic that after spending so long on one I looked forward to getting on another and be stretched out and have all my limbs moved.

They also used to strap me to a tilt table and slowly raised my body at an angle on the table; this helped with circulation and was great to be nearly up right again, being 6ft 4 it took a long time to get used to being at such a low level than I was used to for 25 years.

I had limited mobility in my arms and wanted to get as much mobility back as possible.There was an exercise machine on the wall I would use regularly, because I have no physical grip we had to use bandages to strap my hands on.

There wasn't a lot more physiotherapists could do, so I rotated between hands-on stretching, tilt table and exercise machine.

Occupational therapy was there to help people deal with adjusting to practical issues in order to help people with their new-found disabilities.

They had a machine which I sat in front of consisting of pulleys ropes and weights etc, which supported me by my wrists, it took the weight off and meant I could move my arms more freely.

By combining this with physio after a few months I was able to do some things for myself in a fashion, cleaning my teeth, eating, attempts at shaving, turning pages in magazines or books and using a computer.

I never forget the excitement and feeling of hope and satisfaction the first time I was able to stab a piece of apple and get it to my own mouth although the effort and energy involved was like lifting a dumbbell.

Initially my main goal was to be mobile and to be able to push my own chair. I never developed enough strength or mobility.

Most of the mobility that came back was in my left arm and I was right-handed.

The more realistic option was obviously going to be relying on a power chair for mobility which was an exciting proposal as I would be able to get myself about, and down to the therapy department and to be able to come and go more as I wanted instead of having to rely on pushers.

This proved to be a long exercise firstly getting one I could fit in and then one I could drive.

I got stuck everywhere and crashed into everything, I got stuck in lifts.

I always ran out of stamina and would find myself sat in the corridor waiting for someone to drive the chair for me back to the ward, or I would get myself outside and not be able to get back in.

Looking back it is quite funny but it wasn't at the time it was a very frustrating time. It tested my patience and made me realise how weak, feeble and pathetic I was.

Other people in similar or different situations would try and either push or pull me out places, or move off at 1 mile an hour and try and get help, which often took ages for them to reach their destination as they were as weak as me.

At night I was not allowed to sleep on my back so had to sleep on one side or the other and had to be turned every 3 hours which meant I never got solid sleep, especially when nurses were talking and then janitors would start hoovering around 7 am.

The main thing myself family and friends did learn from occupational therapy was how to get me into a car, as I was like a deadweight.

We had to pull the manual chair next to the car and then one person would swing me around and get my feet inside the car, another person would be steadying me. We then used a sliding board which was a foot wide, about three foot long piece of varnished flat wood, which was placed under my bum and then the two people slid me down into the chair.

Getting into cars wasn't too bad as generally the car was lower than the wheelchair so getting back into the wheelchair was the same process only going uphill which was quite tricky and hard work and quite often I missed the chair and landed on the floor.

Once we had mastered this procedure at weekends I was able to come and go from hospital as I pleased. Which was amazing to be able to go to Meadow hall, cinemas, and pubs, come back to my hometown and generally be able to get out of hospital and have some freedom and fun.

I was also able to visit the family home in Leverton which was amazing to be back in familiar surroundings where I grew up and feel the support from old neighbours and friends.

Overall I was in Sheffield's spinal unit for about eight months and under their care from professional trained doctors and nurses.

I had become quite comfortable and confident expressing what my care needs were although everyone there had plenty of experience working with spinal injury.

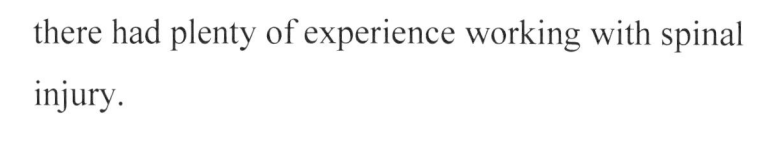

Chapter 5

Nursing home

Whilst in the hospital there was lots of discussions about my future and where I was going to live. I didn't want to go back to living with my dad and didn't want to spend the rest of my life in a nursing home.

There were discussions with social workers about living independently, which was always my hope and desire.

Lots of people around the hospital were trying to make plans for the future.

People said they were living in living rooms or spare rooms whilst their houses were being adapted.

Most people wanting to live independently said it could be a very long drawn-out proces, some people waited months or years to find suitable accommodation depending on their area.

When I left the hospital it was arranged I would spend time in a nursing home in Worksop, until something permanent came up.

I had no idea how long a wait this would be.

After moving into a nursing home where I finally had my own room after 8 months of sharing, which was bliss to be able to sleep without disturbances, have my own TV and music, although I couldn't operate anything myself.

Being in a nursing home was a strange experience; carers and staff would come and go. The food was terrible and usually they had a big meal at dinner and a snack at Tea which I didn't like I prefer the other way around.

Whilst in hospital the only disabilities I have ever really come across were either due to broken necks or backs. Whereas in the nursing home there was a wide range of people with disabilities ranging from brain injury, multiple sclerosis, stroke victims and a wide range of illnesses.

It felt like the kind of place people go to die.

It was a real eye-opener experiencing the darker side of disability, I was getting better and stronger and more confident and it made me appreciate what function I did have. I was especially thankful for my senses my speech and my faculties.

The home was understaffed and it was hard getting the care I needed there were some great carers and people there who did their best to try and entertain people, most of the days everyone was gathered together in the dining room whereas I did often just stay in my room.

At the time I only had my manual wheelchair as the power chair I used in hospital was on loan and I didn't have one yet. Most of the time staff wouldn't have the time or motivation to push me around the grounds.

Due to the turnover of staff I had to learn to articulate my care needs more.

I hated being in that place there was no hope or joy.

For me it was a means to an end.

It was around this time I spent a lot of time thinking about the future and what my options were and what I was going to do with the rest of my life.

Thankfully I had a really good social worker who had arranged for me to see and look at 2 bungalows back in Retford where I wanted to live, as I had always been around the area and had friends there.

I had only been in the nursing home a couple of days when I got to look at 2 properties, both were similar bungalows although one had more of a private garden and the location was better, this is the house I am still living in today.

We still didn't know how long the process would be getting moved in, the turnaround was about four months and I finally moved in January 2001 just over a year after the accident.

It was great thinking of a place which could be called home it was exciting picking out paints and carpets etc.

Whilst in the nursing home I finally had confirmation of moving home, my social worker had sorted out all the benefits I would receive.

It was agreed I would need 24/7 care in order to move home so due to Leonard Cheshire care at home service I started meeting potential carers.

In hospital I had heard of a charity called Back up and arranged a skiing holiday with them, with the intention of starting living independently directly after the holiday.

Part 2; Rolling forward

Chapter 6

Home

I moved into my home in January 2001 the night after my first Sweden skiing holiday, which was great as I went back to the nursing home for one night only and didn't even unpack.

I had met and interviewed carers prior to going to Sweden and had gone through some training with them.

The care agency's shift patterns were starting at 8 o'clock in the morning till 2-30, and then 2-30 till 10 and then a night shift from 10.

This was stupid having carers coming in at 8 in the morning as it was the first time I had a place to call my own and go by my schedule, and there was no way I was getting up at 8 in the morning so they had to try and be quiet on the changeover.

Having a shift change mid-afternoon was also a hindrance as I couldn't go out for the day; it was either a case of going out in the morning and being back or going out after 2-30 unless they were on a double shift.

It was a great feeling going shopping for things for the house, I'd already bought what seemed like a huge TV back in 2001 but could not use it in the nursing home.

I got funding for a computer and had to figure out the best ways of operating one, I found out I was quite capable using a track ball as a mouse and an on-screen keyboard but that is very slow at typing.

I did try cheap versions of dictating software which were rubbish and I never had the patience.

I finally brought a copy of Dragon naturally speaking which I have used ever since. Without the use of the software I wouldn't have been able to get through college, get my degree or be able to write this.

The main problem of using this software is lack of privacy due to everything being spoken out loud, I often feel very self-conscious about what I am saying. If it's nothing personal or confidential it doesn't really matter but whilst writing up personal notes from counselling sessions I often send carers into town or make sure they put the TV on in the carer's room so they can't hear what I am saying.

Often there is no way around the issue so I combine the use of an onscreen keyboard to type key phrases.

The software is very reliable and very accurate although sometimes it is extremely frustrating when it doesn't recognize words or phrases and misinterprets what I have said, I quite often go back through what I have written a few days later and have no idea what the sentence was meant to say, usually though if I sit and write for a couple of hours I am amazed at how much I can write with minimal mistakes.

It was great having sky installed and being able to watch what I wanted when I wanted and to be able to watch films etc.

When I moved in the house I couldn't operate anything. Not the phone, TV or lights everything had to be asked to be done for me.

I had a system put into the house sometime around 2001 which enabled me to operate everything. The system is by a company called RSL steeper.

Initially I had a controller that when I hit a large button it started lights flashing a sequence on the remote and when I reached the right operation allocated I would hit it again and it would perform the operation.

This kit gave me so much independence I am able to operate TV channels and volume, switch channels over to watch a DVD. I can operate the telephone which mutes the TV when answered; it has pre-set numbers so I can dial out.

The house was fitted with an intercom system so I know who is at the door before I let them in. This eventually meant I was safe in the house and could be left alone.

I can open the back door so I can get in and out easier.

In my bedroom I have a profiling bed so I can alter the backrest myself, change the position of the knee break myself and also I have a phone.

At night I operate these from a neck brace and operate everything with my chin.

In hospital they did have similar pieces of kit although much simpler, for example just operating a TV which was down in occupational therapy and it did give me an idea of what is available.

A friend had a similar system installed it was much more expensive and voice activated.

I have an overhead hoist in my bedroom which we have to use for all transfers.

We came up with an ingenious idea of fixing large wheels to the base of reclining chairs which meant I was able to sit in comfort with my feet up, which were actually doctor's orders as it helps with circulation, which is my excuse and I'm sticking to it.

Psychologically and physically I feel more normal when in a normal chair, rather than having to sit in a wheelchair.

This is a bit of trial and error adapting reclining chairs with large wheels.

The last one I bought was just too wide to go through doorways so I had to lose the door going into the living room which was the only option, which has proved to be a nightmare as some carers are noisy at night and now there's no door to shut.

I bought an exercise machine that my feet strapped into which is electric so when it rotates it stretches out my legs the machine raises up so I can strap my hands to it and it exercises my arms, admittedly it only gets used rarely. It feels good at the time but I ache for days afterwards.

I did receive some funding for some equipment I received a shower chair, a bedside table and a drink stand, which has a large flat base and an upright pole which bends of the top at an angle and sits at the side of my chair and holds a cup which does a wonderful job and I would be lost without it but I still can't justify the £160 price tag.

I have a similar one attached to my wheelchair via a bracket and the drink stand swings out when needed and folds away.

(These can be purchased at quality enabling devices.com) It amazes me over the years how many people have commented on the drink stand saying it would be ideal for their son/daughter or whoever can't physically hold a mug or cup and have to ask for a drink every time, which in my position is one of the most frustrating things having to ask for especially when it's a pint of beer.

I have 24/7 care and it took months after being at home before I felt comfortable and safe being on my own , now carers leave around 8 on an evening so I can have some time to myself.

When I moved into the house the back garden was a mess, and literally the only place I could sit was on the ramp which the council had fitted leading into the garden.

The garden became a long-term project and gave me something to focus on and be able to manage, having never had my own garden before this was exciting.

Initially friends built the patio area so I have somewhere to sit, eventually we built a pond. The garden is about the same size of the entire house so really opens things up in the summer.

Figure 1; Me in front of my pond.

Chapter 7

Wheels and transport

Whilst in hospital I had always borrowed a power chair. I did decide to talk to sales reps but everything was very pricey, there were people who had claims who were spending thousands on both manual chairs and power chair especially power chairs. One of my friends at the time bought a power chair for nearly £6000 which I couldn't believe. People were spending between £2000 and £3000 just on manual chairs.

I received a manual chair on the NHS which I used whilst in hospital and in the nursing home.

We were trying to get funding for a power chair which took some time.

I think I received an indoor power chair off the NHS in the first few months of 2001, I was very grateful for this as it gave me more mobility and independence although the battery life was rubbish it only did about a maximum of about 2 miles.

I was so happy to have mobility I went everywhere in that chair and the battery was always going flat, it was great being able to drive myself around parks, garden centres and around town.

I only live about a mile from the town centre and there was no way it could be done in this chair so we needed to find a vehicle capable of carrying myself in the power chair, these really did cost thousands of pounds.

A friend of my brother's was selling an old ambulance for about £500, so we went up and had a look at it and it was perfect.

The vehicle was very high so we had to buy telescopic ramps which extended to about 10 feet. A company called Clarke and Partners fitted tracks inside and we bought clamps to secure the chair to the ambulance and a safety harness to keep me secure.

Overall we spent about a thousand pounds on the ambulance and at the time it was great, it meant no more transfers into cars and I could go out with just 1 person instead of needing 2.

Due to the size of the ambulance and the telescopic ramps we needed about a 20 foot parking space which was a nightmare, as was extending the telescopic ramps as they were so heavy and had to be physically put into place.

The ambulance itself had a 3 L engine and was a V6 which meant it was very thirsty on fuel and cost a fortune to go anywhere.

One of my carers husband's works at a garage and they had a bus go to the garage for repairs which had an electric tail lift on the back in full working order which they didn't want, so I paid £150 for it and had it fitted on the back of the ambulance which made life so much easier to drive onto the tail lift and carers operated it and I rose to the right level to drive into the ambulance.

I used the ambulance for about a year it did serve the purpose and with it being so large I even slept in it.

During this time my father set up a trust fund for me and put some money away so the first two purchases we looked into was a power chair and a better more suitable vehicle.

I tried a few different power chairs some of which were mental, extremely fast and uncontrollable. One sales rep showed me a chair out of the house and didn't even bother adjusting anything on it to make it more comfortable and fitting. I quite liked the chair but his attitude was terrible and I didn't want to give him thousands of pounds.

I had read reviews about a power chair called a Jazzy 1151 by a company called Pride mobility and I was excited to try a demo model, this sales rep was friendly and patient. I got hoisted into the chair and he made lots of adjustments so it fitted perfectly, he came out for a good walk with me and told me to give it a good testing up and down curbs and over different terrains, in out of the house and the chair was perfect it handled everything and felt completely stable it had power and an amazing turning circle, due to being mid wheel drive.

The chair cost £3500 and was worth every penny I haven't needed to buy another power chair since it has had plenty of repairs though.

We also started looking for a better vehicle of which there are a few on the market we decided on a 1.9 L diesel Renault Kangoo which we had specifically adapted with a ramp in the back which just unfolds, I drive into the vehicle the chair is clamped to the floor and a seatbelt is put on and away we go.

The van has been a godsend; cheap to run, very practical and has luxuries like radio and heating which the ambulance didn't, although now it is very dated and still has a tape deck. When I bought the van I used to fill the tank for £20 now it costs around £45.

I always keep a little aluminium ramp in my van which was bought for £30 from Netto of all places which comes in very handy getting up kerbs and into people's houses. The big long expensive telescopic ones were about £400 and were useless for day to day use.

Having the combination of a powerful outdoor chair which does about 25 miles on paper and an accessible vehicle meant there were literally no limits to where and how far I could travel.

I still have this vehicle and power chair and they have both proved their worth and have done miles.

Chapter 8

Hiring and firing

At first the spinal hospital were responsible for my care and then due to being in a nursing home it became their responsibility. When I first moved home in 2001 carers were supplied by a service called Leonard Cheshire care home service.

I used this the first year or so it was their responsibility to sort out shifts, wages tax etc.

The services folded so it was either find another agency or take more charge myself, I heard about the independent living scheme which enables people to take more control of their care team by paying the service user directly and I already had a team in place.

The first thing we decided as a team was to change the shift pattern and decided to break it down to 12 hour shifts, 10 AM to 10 PM for a day shift and vice versa for a night shift.

One of the carers Dawn who was the very first person on the first shift eventually took the role of senior carer and started organising shift patterns which she still does 10 years on, we do have some kind of system but shifts are always getting changed to work around individuals as some prefer doing double shifts as it cuts down on petrol costs and also gives them more time at home.

The downside of being more independent is that it is my responsibility to advertise and interview as required and it is down to me to fire people if necessary as quite often things don't work out.

I employ 5 people 3 of which are full-time and 2 are part-time there is no fall back if people are ill the shifts still need covering usually it works pretty well and people help each other out.

Legally being the employer brings all the fun tasks like tax and national insurance. It has the benefit due to me being responsible for paying the wages advances can be made throughout the month if necessary either in cash or by the Internet.

Firing people is never fun or pleasant but unfortunately it goes with the territory, if people aren't pulling their weight or doing their job or not turning up or coming in drunk then a decision has to be made.

Quite often it is their decision to leave and it is agreed they work a month extra or until a replacement is found.

Interviewing is the better part of the process as I can try and figure people out and see if we'll get on and see if they're suitable.

I have had the same team for about five years now but when advertising and starting the process I have had all kinds of people asking for work ranging from qualified nurses, skilled carers to fruit pickers or people that haven't done any work in care.

Chapter 9

Reiki and spirituality

Once I had settled in at home I started looking into alternative therapies which would help me heal or help maintain my health.

I didn't know how to decorate my house and became interested in crystal healing so my decorations and ornaments were mainly crystal. I do believe they have some therapeutic value, there was one particular stone which was rose quartz which always made me feel different when I was close to it.

I think at that time I was willing to try anything in order to heal.

I read about Reiki which interested me and a friend's mother Lorna was a master so I gave it a try.

Reiki is a hands-on healing which does not involve actual touch but she transfers energy to where it is needed and it cleanses the chakras and flushes out toxins.

I am very sensitive and attuned to this and treatments are extremely relaxing. I often see swirling masses of vibrant colour deep inside my consciousness and at that moment of high awareness I feel my mind going somewhere else this is especially strong if outside and soaking up all the natural energy.

When I first started having treatments a lot of sensations were quite alien to me and limited throughout my body and I found myself concentrating and focusing on where she was working whilst shutting my eyes, initially I was not very self-aware but over time and whilst studying anatomy I have been able to visualize internally and map out more clearly my body and imagine the energy flowing through organs and muscle groups.

I have kept on having treatments 10 years on every couple of weeks or so. I feel it helps me unwind and de-stress and helps keep me healthy, I very rarely get ill other than colds and have very little to do with my GP and I haven't spoken to the spinal consultant for years.

I feel the body is just a vessel carrying consciousness and when the body dies consciousness does remain. I would like to believe that when I do die my consciousness will be reunited with my mother's, especially after the accident and hearing the words "not yet" I can't explain if it was a connection with the afterlife and I hope it is a long time before I get this question answered.

Chapter 10

Music and live entertainment

A major advantage of being a wheelchair user is availability of tickets for concerts and live entertainment, a lot of the time I have a separate booking number for customers with special needs and requirements especially at Sheffield Hallam arena, when the tickets go on sale there is no messing around waiting to get through to the box office I can easily get through first or second time.

I quite often get lucky phoning up two or three weeks after tickets have gone on sale and there are still some left in wheelchair bays.

The arena itself is fantastic for wheelchair users I'm guaranteed a good view no matter where I sit. I share a bay with other wheelchair users and have an excellent view and always feel safe with no one dancing and bashing into the chair like people do in pubs. I quite often find that my carers will get a concession and get in free to certain events so we split the price between us.

I got extremely lucky last year and filled in the ballot for Wimbledon and managed to get front row tickets for the women's semi-final on Court 1. Which was an amazing view unfortunately it rained so we saw our match on Court 1 and then due to my situation and circumstance we managed to blag ourselves into centre court, we were in the rafters but it was nice having a bonus of seeing a semi-final match on centre court.

The only time I remember having a bad view was at the Arctic Monkeys at Manchester Cricket ground, and the bay for wheelchairs was completely the other end of the ground to the stage and the view was terrible. I'm usually very lucky and get to sit in front for most events.

Live music is a great distraction, the only frustrating thing for me is not being able to clap and applaud a good performance which is a very strange feeling.

I try to go to 2 or three different events a year I recently saw the Chinese state circus and was in awe of the skill and beauty and precision of the acrobats whilst juggling or dancing.

I saw the Circus of horrors show recently which was quite disturbing and entertaining it consisted of freaks eating glass, juggling fire and knives, swallowing swords and a dwarf lifting a bowling ball with his penis, some things in life you don't need to see.

Last year I went to see Jeff Wayne's musical version of War of the Worlds which was that good I am going again this year it had a 50 piece band a 100ft cgi screen a 15ft floating head and a very large fire breathing Martian this was very entertaining.

Most cinemas have a policy of letting the carer get in free too so we split the cost so going to the cinema isn't as expensive for both of us, we also have the luxury of going mid-day when it's quiet.

Chapter 11

Walk a mile in my shoes

In order to be able to understand another person's being and to be empathetic means imagining what it would be like for you being that person and seeing things from their perspective.

How many tasks and routines do you do for yourself on a daily basis? How much do you take for granted? How would it feel to have to rely on someone else for these basic functions? How would you feel if you knew you will never walk again? How would you feel if you had very limited and restricted movement?

I have an iPod alarm clock which is set about half an hour before the next carer comes on shift so I can listen to the music and wake up gradually, or not depending on what's on.

Sometimes when I sleep my unconscious mind is able-bodied and I quite often dream that I am able and capable, sometimes I wake up and forget I am paralysed and think right time to get up and start the day then I remember that I can't get off the bed.

In order to get a carer's attention in the morning I usually put the living room light on from my bedroom or I set the phone off.

First thing is having some water as my throat is very dry in the morning, I usually need sleep wiping from my eyes. Most mornings these are part of the routine but quite often I still have to ask as they are starting the main morning routine.

If it's just a normal morning I have a wipe down or a bed wash as I have a shower and do my toileting every other day.

Some mornings I wake up and the convene has leaked so am covered in piss which is never a good way to start a day.

The night bag is emptied and swapped over to a leg bag. If it's a fresh one the valve needs to be checked it is shut otherwise it goes all over the carpet, which has happened far too many times for it to be funny. On a normal morning I have one carer and usually on shower mornings we use two.

I need rolling in order to get my trousers up which sometimes takes 2 or 3 rolls. I don't wear boxers as they get bunched up and get very uncomfortable.

Putting socks on always seems a bit of a chore as the natural way is to pull them up yourself whereas on me they need pushing up.

I then need to get in the sling, Some people roll me from side to side and bunch the sling up and pull it under me, some people sit me up either with the backrest of the bed or embracing my body and with assistance I have enough strength to sit up and the sling is rolled down my back.

I am then hoisted into either my power chair if I am going out or the armchair if I'm just at home.

The hoist has 4 buttons up and down, left and right and these often get pressed incorrectly so I end up all over the place. sometimes I get sat perfectly first-time, other times I need repositioning in the chair usually back and to the right so my bum is straight this is usually done by pulling me back with my trousers which bunch up at the crotch so they need un bunching and straightening up which sometimes pulls me forward this can often take 3 or 4 attempts.

Most of the time I don't get hit by the overhead hoist but quite often it hits me in the face or head and is very heavy.
If it is a shower morning 9 times out of 10 we have 2 carers on for safety when I am wet.
I get hoisted onto the shower chair first and have enemas inserted up my bum and am manually checked.

Usually it is a quick process but sometimes I am constipated and they can take up to an hour which usually involves lots of prodding and poking which isn't a very good way to start the day.

I am then showered and dressed. On a normal morning around 20 minutes is ample to get me off the bed. If it is a shower and toilet morning we always pencil in around an hour.

Normally I get up around 10 so time isn't an issue, if I have to be somewhere at a certain time I usually give myself an hour and a half this usually takes in to account having to shave, cleaning my teeth and a cup of tea.

Most carers have their own way of working and when they are paired up some people's styles complement each other and they work well together, each doing their own part of the routine and not getting each other's way so it goes as smooth as clockwork other times they completely clash and are in each other's way and repeating tasks and not paying attention to what the other has already done, for example going to fetch something from the bathroom and the other person already has it and it seems to take forever to get up and dressed and off the bed.

It is often a frustrating process picking what clothes to wear as I have to say which pair of trousers I want and most look the same when all pulled out together usually I just agree on which ever pair I can see unless I need to be smart and presentable so I need to be more specific. It is very annoying finding clothes unpresentable and not ironed stuffed in the wardrobe; an able-bodied person would not wear them so I don't see why I should.

One reoccurring theme which still happens 12 years on is when I say; can you do something to my left or right. For example repositioning and carers get the wrong one because they are facing opposite. When I say left I mean my left obviously, when this happens I usually respond with; no my other left! Winds me up.

Some mornings I am chatty throughout the process other times I just leave them to get on with it and just keep an eye on the process. Some mornings carers are chatty which sometimes helps the routine go quicker other times I really can't be arsed to listen to chitchat or gossip first thing in the morning so just listen to the music.

I have had a few carers over the years and it's often difficult completely trusting them when there is no middle ground or common interests other than their job is looking after me, but I have no escape and often get life stories first thing in the morning and have to go into counselling mode.

If I have plans for the day or the morning I will get in my power chair and put the TV on until time to go out or if I have no plans I will get in my armchair and go on the computer for whatever reason.

I only really start to feel more myself once I am up and sat.

The first thing I can really do for myself is cleaning my teeth, I have a adapted Velcro strap which holds a toothbrush, some mornings I still have to ask to clean my teeth.

I never have breakfast and usually wait till dinner to have a snack or if I have something on in the morning I will eat afterwards. I need feeding all meals. I always drink loads throughout the day and am constantly asking for drinks, all of which need drinking through a straw ; Tea, Beer, soup, squash whatever the worst one is champagne it is horrible through a straw as is wine and spirits but thankfully I don't drink these often.

I generally do my own shopping unless it's just a few bits and pieces which need picking up whereas it would be more hassle for me to go along.

I don't particularly like doing shopping so physically get as much as possible whilst I am there. I quite often go with the same carer to the same shop and it is quite a smooth process, sometimes it isn't.

I very often find it difficult to look into the freezers due to being at a lower level so have to ask what's in there; it can often be quite difficult communicating what I want to pick up.

I often find it difficult looking up to the higher shelves also to be able to read what the products are, especially seeing prices and sell by dates which are also hard to monitor as some people grab whatever's at the front and are not patient enough to get fresher products from the back.

I always forget after a week or so what I have purchased so have to ask what is in the fridge or freezer, not being able to physically look myself often leads to food being wasted.

It is also difficult judging how much space there is in the freezer and how much too buy. Normally I don't get it to wrong but there have been times I've completely misjudged it and ended up with 10 or so items that won't fit in the freezer.

When I want something from the freezer I have to ask them to describe what's in there or if there is something specifically I want that I remember buying I ask for that and carers have to rummage around in the freezer.

The good thing for me is that once I have been to the supermarket, my job is done and I don't have to put it all away. Different carers will put things in different places which always causes confusion.

Throughout the day it often feels like I am being babysat as there is always someone around and I ask them to help or for assistance as required.

On an evening if carers are working just a day shift I let them go home at 8 o'clock instead of 10.

I get set up with a couple of drinks on the table and keep my mouse on my lap so I can still use a computer whilst watching TV.

Quite often I have to ask for a few things to be done at the same time so feel as though I'm giving out around 10 orders at once usually I try and ask for things step-by-step.

I can't even count throughout the day how many times I am asking for assistance I try to be as polite as possible but don't always remember the please and thank you.

I quite often find myself asking a carer to do something and then I leave it with them and find I have to ask again in a few hours to see if it the task has been done.

I recently had to ask 3 different carers 3 different times just to post a set of films back. It's gets repetitive and monotonous asking for the same things on a daily basis.

When I am counselling, coaching, studying or whatever I am involved in at that time carers do their own thing and leave me to it, I prefer to use different support networks depending on what I'm doing for example whilst studying I use their support workers and whilst coaching I rely more on different team members. I feel it is important to separate the 2 and keep carers for care needs.

One reoccurring theme is having carers around whilst going out for a meal with family, friends or women. I need assistance with feeding so usually carers come along but sometimes I just want to spend time on my own with whomever and have some privacy so the awkward question of who is feeding comes up.

Quite often a family member will take over and finish with me if they have done as it takes longer feeding 2 people than 1.

It is awkward if just with a women and asking them to feed me too but it's better than having a carer sat at the table also.

At parties I generally go on my own and my mates will give me some snap and get me drunk. A lot of people stare which bothered me at first it's just another thing to adapt to.

At the end of each day I'm given my nightly medication, I self-medicate with beer but not so much during the week.

My chair is pulled into the bedroom. Usually it is easier to take off jumpers, T-shirts, wrist supports whilst I'm still sat.

I am hoisted onto the bed and undressed fully. I wear a collar around my neck which enables me to set the bed up so that I am comfy; I always put the TV on and finish watching the programme before I go to sleep. Getting to bed is a quick process and takes between 10 and 15 minutes.

At night I usually sleep okay but it is very frustrating when I can't sleep and can't roll about, I alter the backrest on the bed and the knee break on my bed to change position.

I often feel very trapped inside my body and just think.

If I am desperate for a drink I will wake a carer and have some water usually once I am put to bed I don't see anyone till morning.

Nights are very lonely and boring if I can't sleep. Carers usually go to sleep themselves but some don't go to bed until later, I have headphones for the TV but quite often do not get a good night's sleep due to carers being awake making noise in the middle of the night.

One huge difference to being a wheelchair user than being able-bodied is spatial awareness, I always have to look forward and plan my route more looking out for flat curbs which the chair can get down. Likewise for getting up curbs, I quite often have to go out of my way to find access points.

I always have to scan the terrain and make sure the chair will go over it in order to pick the best route that the chair will be able to cope with, sometimes it is uneven on a slope or a camber the chair becomes more difficult to drive.

If there are large obstacles in the way a new route has to be picked.

I always tend to go backwards down larger ramps or a slope due to the way the chair is balanced so there is no fear of tipping forward.

Quite often I see people in chairs going forward down slopes out of control and it doesn't look safe.

I always have to be aware of people around me as people often don't look down so I have to second-guess which way they are going.

I always have to assess buildings, houses and shops etc. to make sure there aren't any steps and the doors are wide enough for the chair to fit through.

I always need to make sure the chair has enough charge for a planned visit, I do carry a spare cable in my rucksack at all times just in case it does run out of charge if this happens it's usually a case of finding a pub and plugging into the mains. How would you feel if you had to take more awareness of your environment?

Money becomes a bit of a strange concept when you can't physically handle it yourself. How would you feel putting your trust in others to deal with your money?

A lot of my banking is done online and I have absolute control over this, everything else I have to rely on carers. When things are purchased they deal with money it does get difficult to manage how much is in my wallet at any given time, I quite often have times when I go to the shop, or somebody else goes and my cash card has not been replaced back in my wallet so I end up stuck with no money.

I have had times in the past when amounts just haven't added up and there is an element of doubt.

Initially I had to explain to my bank about my injury and the fact that my signature would change, which they were okay with and accommodating but my signature is worse than that of a child's so does quite often get questioned on cheques or documents. To say it is easy to copy is an understatement.

Initially I felt quite guilty about claiming benefits and it took some getting used to it becomes strange appreciating the value of it knowing that if I buy something too expensive or go over budget then a week or 2 more money will be put in.

I am not driven by money at all although it is nice earning more when you prove your worth, I am well looked after financially which is why I don't mind to a certain extent giving up and volunteering my time for coaching or counselling within reason although I still have to maintain and run a vehicle.

I use direct payments to pay for the care and tax and insurance. I'm used to paying large amounts out at once but it is a lot of responsibility making sure tax and national insurance are paid as are wages; there is lots of temptation when dealing with such large amounts. It usually always runs smoothly but becomes a panic when it runs low.

One thing that really does wind me up is when I run out of medication. Tablets are sent out via the chemist on a monthly basis as well as everything else which I have to order.

On the same day which just happened to be a bank holiday I was told I had run out of diazepam which helps me sleep and relax the spasm in my legs. When I went to the toilet in the morning I found out I had no enemas which make me go to the toilet. It is the first time ever running out of them but surely over the last week or so 1 out of 5 carers should have noticed we were running low and mentioned it so would be able to order some more.

I do check the stock myself when phoning through an order but I am not psychic or a mind reader so I should have been told we were running low.

Figure 2; My family on my mums side.

Part 3; Rolling around the world

Chapter 12

Back-up -Skiing

I first heard about a charity called the Back-up trust early on in my injury.

Back Up was founded in 1986 by the former British and European Freestyle Champion and James Bond stunt double Mike Nemesvary, who was an aerial skier who broke his neck during a stunt and wanted to get back up the mountain and ski again, it is a charity whose aim is to improve confidence, self-esteem and independence after spinal injury and get people involved in outdoor activities.

Whilst in hospital and on bed rest a friend of mine had made a large collage from my favourite photos which ranged from skateboarding, snowboarding, mountain biking and various activities holidays and friends etc.

This was always a talking point and focus point and it made me think of all the good times I had experienced.

One of the nurses talked about a skiing trip she was about to go on to Sweden, as a carer and said there would be six wheelchair users who are paralysed at some level.

I was sceptical and thought good for them, how would I be able to ski again when I can't walk or feed myself or dress myself.

When she got back she showed me photos and a video and said there was a chap very similar to myself in injury and they got him skiing and he said it was the best week of his life.

I jumped at the opportunity and signed up for next winter as it had to be at least 12 months after injury.

This gave me something to focus on and dream about and something to hope for.

When January 2001 finally came it was an amazing feeling packing for a winter holiday as snowboarding had always been a passion of mine.

I had so many questions. What would the ski kart be like? How will I cope with the cold? How would I be able to steer and control? How do I get on the plane? How would flying agree with me? Would I get the same excitement as boarding? And most importantly how fast will they go?

The group met at a disabled water-ski facility near Heathrow there were six wheelchair users, six nurses or carers and a few people called buddies who were there to help with lifting, pushing and helping people with coats and gloves etc.

I was so full of excitement and anxiety I was sick which seemed to be happening all the time early on. Once I got chatting to people I was fine.

Once it was time to board the plane wheelchair users were first on and last off.

They wheeled the chair near to the cockpit I was lifted from the wheelchair to an aisle chair and then lifted into a plane seat.

The rest of the flight I felt like a normal traveller.

The ski kart itself was a great piece of kit there was a plastic shell where you sat with your feet up in front so there was no worry of balance, the kart is quite wide with a low centre of gravity it had two fixed skis at the back and two skis at the front which were attached to the levers on the side of the cart.

The first morning was trying to get the tension right so I could operate the skis.

They also had gloves with buckles on to grip handles. The kart was designed to use standard T-bar drag lifts which hook onto the front.

There was an instructor tethered to the back of the cart to help control speed and act as a brake. The aim was to get skiing independently.

I couldn't believe I was skiing again the sense of excitement and adrenaline was intense especially being so low to the ground, the sensation of carving and turning was wonderful and it was amazing to soak up all the views.

It was like a whole new world of freedom and independence and I soon found out they went very fast.

The first year I went was just about having fun and blowing off steam as I got tired very quickly so was only really out on the snow for a couple of hours a day.

I managed to go back another 2 times and by the end of the third holiday I was let off the rope at the top of certain runs and the instructor would race me down to the bottom, they put out slalom poles and I was quite capable of weaving in and out.

The most important thing apart from the actual skiing was interacting and socialising with people who have had injuries some time ago and finding out how they coped, how they have adapted, what problems may arise and how to deal with them. Finding out if and how they have been accepted by society or rejected by people.

Likewise talking to nurses and buddies about how they view disability and people with spinal cord injury gave me more insight.

I also experienced two magical experiences which I would never have expected and are once-in-a-lifetime experiences.

One was a dog sleigh ride which was fast and exhilarating, the other was a reindeer sleigh ride which was slow and peaceful down in the snowy valleys of

Sweden surrounded by frozen lakes and snowy scenes which was very picturesque.

Some of the sleighs did topple over which must have been awful for a tetraplegic or paraplegic person falling off in the snow although it was quite funny to watch, thankfully I managed to stay on, which made me chuckle as usually if anyone would fall off into the snow it would be me.

After the first year this improved my confidence, independence and self-esteem and I came back a different person.

Figure 3; The ski kart.

Figure 4;Reindeer ride.

Figure 5;Sweden views.

Chapter 13

Back up -multi-activity

Back up also offered multi-activity weeks in the summer in Keswick in the Lake District which has always been one of my favourite places in Britain.

In 2002 I was keen to see what else I could do.

I went sailing, canoeing and out on a catamaran all of which were new experiences. Getting in and out of boats we relied on brute force and ignorance which took some trust and was like leaps of faith and I hoped I wouldn't get dropped in the water. It was all new to me but the guys knew what they were doing.

Going out on a catamaran was amazing it was just a shame there was not much wind and we didn't get to full speed.

It was impressive seeing all the adapted kit and filled me with hope.

The activity centre even had an assault course especially designed for wheelchairs which consisted of bridges, narrow things to get across seesaws etc. which was great fun although I couldn't push the chair I had to direct the pusher.

One of my best memories from Back up involved a weekend in Wales Quad biking.

I was lifted into the Quad bike and I think we used gaffer tape to fix my hands to the steering wheel.

The Quad bike had been adapted so inside my helmet I had a pipe in my mouth and when I sucked on the pipe the vehicle accelerated and when I blew down it decelerated.

I was with other people on quad bikes but it was amazing to be able to hack around the base of Snowdon driving over rocks and logs, dodging trees in woods and driving through mud and small rivers completely independently.

I became good friends with one of the group leaders and for about 3 years I would travel around various spinal hospitals and give a talk with her about my experiences with Back up and the impact it has had on my life.

Hopefully whilst these people were still in hospital they gave some thought about participating themselves.

The Back up trust is not government funded and is a charity, we used to pay about a third of the cost of holidays and the rest is funded by them.

One of the ways they did fundraising was through skydiving which I always wanted to try; the doctors did reluctantly sign a consent form and thought I was mad wanting to do it.

I raised nearly £350. On the day of the jump we discussed safety and landing and how I would be caught on the ground.

It was a really windy day and no one jumped we were sat around most of the day until we were sent home.

I got a phone call the next day saying the instructors had decided not to let me do it which was gutting especially having raised so much money on paper.

I'm a believer in things happening for a reason or not, and decided jumping out of a plane probably wasn't the best idea so didn't look into it again.

My mate did do one he said it was amazing and he did raise some money.

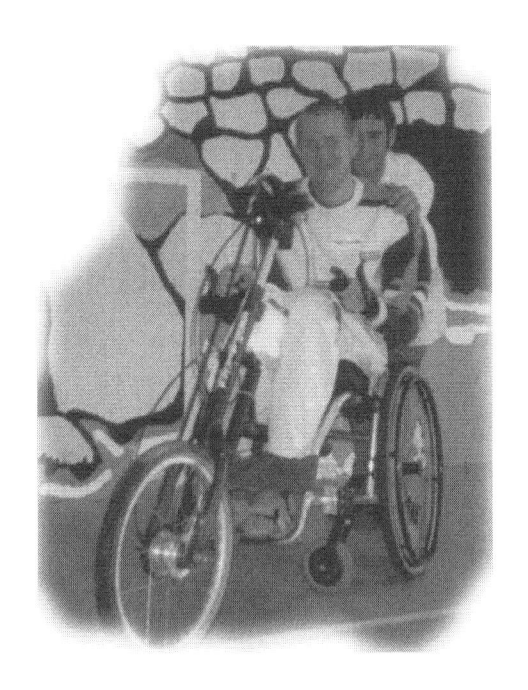

Figure 6;On a hand bike.

Figure 7;Wheelchair assault course .

Figure 8;Canoeing.

Figure 9;Sailing.

Figure 10;Going out on a Catamaran.

Chapter 14

Egypt

Egypt was always a place I fancied visiting but never had the opportunity.

I have been very lucky regarding Back up and skiing holidays regarding finances, if I wanted to go again I wouldn't have been able to get assistance with payment so would have been looking at paying full price for myself and a carer or 2, travelling with Back up they also supply the care.

I decided if my next holiday would cost a lot of money I wanted a different experience so I suggested Egypt to my father in 2006 and he agreed with the idea and surprised me by saying he would like to come along with his partner.

We decided it would be best if I took 2 carers.

I thought with it being an once-in-a-lifetime experience I wanted to do it properly and Accessible travel who I had booked with offered a cruise down the Nile and a luxury hotel in Cairo.

It was the first time travelling independently and Accessible travel had assured us we would have a wheelchair accessible taxi from the airport, we would be able to get on and off boats and they would supply a pusher and I would be able to get around temples, pyramids etc.

Taking my power chair was never an option so I had to rely on my manual chair and people to push me around.

I travelled with my carers and arranged to meet my father in Cairo.

The original plan was to get to Cairo and spend a few days in a hotel and then work our way back down the Nile but the itinerary got complicated and it was arranged we would go down the Nile first, it was a very long journey and they took us sightseeing as soon as we arrived and it was around 48 hours being awake from leaving home.

If we would have had the hotel for a few days first it would have been brilliant as we could have relaxed and got used to the heat.

Cruising down the Nile was extremely relaxing and we stopped off at various temples on the way including the Temple of Hatshepsut, Luxor, Karnak, the Aswan dam. I saw the unfinished obelisk and then finished up in Cairo to see the pyramids and the Museum of Cairo. Other than seeing the pyramids the Museum was my favourite thing to see, actually seeing all the artefacts that have been found over the years especially seeing the Tutankhamen collection was breath-taking.

The company weren't lying when they said that they would get me around as much as possible. The Valley of the Kings was out of the question other than that they got me everywhere I wanted to go, we were all grateful for having pushers even the locals were dripping sweat due to the 35-45 degrees scorching temperatures and I wasn't sure how I would cope with the heat and at times it was unbearable.

These guys must have loved us though we were tipping roughly the equivalent of a British fiver for an hour or so work, we later found out about a British tenner was equivalent to a week's wage for them.

I brought back with me some lovely papyrus pictures, ornaments and a 3ft carved granite obelisk (somehow) so my living room is all Egyptian .

Whilst on the Nile cruise ships would moor up side-by-side so the only way to get on land was by going through the other ships, the entrance was never in the same position so I had 4 or more Egyptians who couldn't speak or understand English trying to balance the chair on very tight lips on the boat exteriors.

How no one ended up in the water is beyond me.

Egypt isn't renowned for wheelchair access and whenever we came to stairs I would try and explain part of the chair came to bits, next thing I would know was that the chair was being lifted up 20 or so steps which was pretty scary, as was getting on and off the boat as their idea of a bridge was 2 old pieces of wood.

Most of the time I did shut my eyes and hoped I would get either on dry land or back on the boat without either coming out the chair or ending up in the water, thankfully that never happened.

It was certainly worth the risk and I will never forget seeing the great Pyramids with my father.

Figure 11;Me and my Dad at the great pyramid.

Figure 12; At Luxor.

Figure 13; Some Egyptian statues.

Chapter 15

Holidays

The Egypt holiday was a success but was an once-in-a-lifetime opportunity certainly from a financial viewpoint. I really enjoyed relaxing in the sun but wanted something a bit nearer and cheaper so I decided on Gran Canaria.

I used the same booking agency as they had delivered last time and they offered a 4-star hotel at a reasonable price with a nearby promenade.

I arranged for the hire of a hoist and shower chair which was waiting at the hotel upon our arrival. Accessible Travel arranged for a wheelchair taxi to take us from the airport to the hotel and then we fended for ourselves for the week.

Taking 2 carers was the only real option; once I am up and about I only really need help with food and drink.

Carers are there if I need them we decided the best way was to divide the entire week's work between the 2, I paid for the majority of the holiday and got some back from what they would have earned, which I used as my spending money.

This was the first time I had flown with my power chair, there was no way I was relying on using a manual chair for a week it wasn't so bad in Egypt as we were on boats and looking around temples which weren't accessible. I like to come and go as I please and go for wanders on my own.

I was worried about how my power chair would be handled and ignorance is bliss we saw them at the airport bashing it around and nearly dropping it whilst getting it off the conveyor.

It was a completely new experience going on holiday with no agenda or nothing to do and was great just to be able to relax, sit by pools and read or listen to an iPod although extremely frustrating not being able to just jump in the water and swim or soak and cool down. It was successful with no calamities.

I now have used the same tour agency 4 times and have had no problems with them at all, every time we have had a wheelchair accessible taxi from the airport and been able to hire a hoist, shower chairs and mattresses.

I have been to Lanzarote where we hired a self-catering apartment and to Cyprus where we hired a villa which slept six of us. I like to be near the sea which usually means there are nice smooth promenades to roll down.

Cyprus was okay for access although there was lots of large curbs we were quite lucky to be on the main bus route to Pathos so we could jump on a bus and head up to the bars and restaurants or continue on to the harbour city of Pathos, this was great the buses had built in ramps which folded out and it was no problem getting on and off.

I really enjoyed Cyprus there was a good mixture of time spent relaxing around the Villa and there were plenty of temples, museums and archaeological sites to explore although there were many restrictions on where I could actually get in a wheelchair.

My brother was the one that went off exploring and took lots of photos and video clips so I could still see everything although virtually.

Figure 14;Oh I do like to be besides the sea.

Figure 15;Me and Dad in Cyprus.

Chapter 16

Norfolk

My father moved down to Norfolk a couple of years after myself and my brother were settled in houses as his partner lived there and my father was doing some work on some boats.

I have been there and stayed with them 3 or 4 times.

The first few times I stayed at a nearby hospital which had all the facilities and nurses at hand so I used the place as a B&B so during the day I would spend time with my father and Gill. This worked out really well as I was able to get my care needs at the hospital and throughout the day all that is needed is general assistance.

It also gave me a break from my carers and them a break from me, we arranged to swap vehicles halfway so we would have the use of my van whilst in Norfolk.

The last time I went down I stayed at the Leonard Cheshire care home on Sandringham estate where Diana grew up which had been fully adapted as a hotel and had excellent equipment, good food and beautiful surroundings the only downside was the bar shut around nine o'clock. On an evening it was like a ghost town with no one about.

While in Norfolk we would always make sure to visit the surrounding stately homes, museums, Sea Life Centres and possibly the best zoos I have seen in this country, I love seeing animals especially when they're in good environments and are well looked after.

We also hired a couple of different wheelchair accessible boats on the Norfolk Broads; I always enjoy the sensation of being on boats and on the water.

My father's friends own a 4-man Cessna plane, which was extremely difficult getting me in as I had to be lifted from the chair onto the wing and then from the wing into the plane but was certainly worth the hassle being in such a small plane and flying so low over the east coast of Anglia and seeing from the sky various places we have visited.

Figure 16;On the Norfolk broads.

Chapter 17

Free as a bird

One thing I always wanted to try but never got the opportunity was to go up in a glider. I looked into this around 2005 and went up to a local airstrip and asked if I would be able to go up, I explained my condition and most of the pilots weren't too keen on the idea.

Thankfully an experienced pilot was willing to give it a go.

I found getting into the glider was a ball ache as there wasn't a hoist and wasn't much space so we relied on manpower, brute force and ignorance using 4 men.

Once I was in hitting the joystick with my legs became a safety concern and obviously I didn't want to be knocking it and putting myself and the pilot in danger.

We took off my trainers and used them to tie around my knees to the framework so that there was no chance of knocking anything.

We used a mechanical launcher and the plane was catapulted into the air which surprised me at the amount of force and my stomach felt like it was on a roller coaster.

Once we were up in the air it was simply stunning there was no sound whatsoever and the plane really shook about in the wind, it was a lovely clear bright day with plenty of thermals so we stayed in the air for about 45 minutes.

The airstrip was about 5 miles from where I live so it was amazing to fly over my home, Clumber Park and local areas.

It really was a feeling of freedom just flying around. It would have been nice to have enough movement to have been able to control the plane but it was enough just being in the air with no noise.

The descent was extremely scary especially when he was trying to lose momentum and speed and he came down with a real bump.

I have never before felt so free.

I always enjoy new experiences and will never forget this, I love anything where I can leave the chair behind and this was extremely special.

Part 4; Rolling backwards

Chapter 18

Mishaps

There have been a few mishaps over the years of things which are not expected that made me realise weaknesses and how vulnerable I am.

In hospital whilst trying out chairs my father and brother took me out around the hospital grounds and through some woods, the cushion I sat on wasn't fixed down so somehow over the bumps I managed to slide and fall out of the chair. This was in the early days and we weren't sure the best ways of lifting, it was a case of one person lifting my legs and the other under my arms and lifting me back into the chair, it was an early lesson in making sure the cushion is fixed.

During the time in the nursing home where I had an ensuite bathroom thankfully, the carers stayed in my bedroom whilst I was in the toilet and somehow whilst sat on a shower chair my body went into spasm and physically threw me forward head first onto the floor and due to having limited mobility in my arms I wasn't able to protect myself from falling. This terrified me and made me feel so helpless. I still don't know how this happened I couldn't throw myself forward if I tried.

Shower chairs are not the most stable equipment and all come in different shapes and sizes. I strapped myself onto them for quite a while just to feel safe.

I trust the one I have at home but I'm always dubious about using ones on loan in hospitals, nursing homes and especially on holiday.

While I was at college in 2002 having a classroom upstairs I used the same lift frequently.

I had a different power chair back then which wasn't mid wheel drive the steering was from the front wheels. I started driving into the lift and didn't notice that the level of the lift was about 6 inches below the level of the floor so drove into the lift; my carer had gone up the stairs to operate it so I only had my academic support worker with me.

I drove into the lift and my front wheels went over the lip which threw me head first onto the floor and then the power chair fell on top of me.

My academic support worker at the time was a tiny lady so she ran upstairs to find my carer who came back down to find me in a heap with a power chair on top of me, this really worried me and I went to hospital for an x-ray of my neck which was okay. I didn't fancy doing any more damage to myself; it would have been just my luck doing more damage to my neck whilst falling into a lift.

I learnt to be cautious every time I go into a lift and make sure the floor is level, it took me a while to get over this phobia and I'm still not really a fan of lifts which is a strange thing when I have to rely on them all the time.

I didn't want to use lifts for a while but had no choice. The college did replace this particular lift. I tried making a claim against them for neglect but because I didn't physically hurt myself apart from a strained ankle, apparently someone worrying about damaging their neck after already breaking it isn't enough to make a claim although the psychological trauma for me lasted quite a while.

There was one lift I came across at Cairo airport which was knackered to say the least and I refused to go in it, I made the airport officials walk me all the way around the airport.

I nearly also fell into a boat in Norfolk which had a tail lift attached to the back and lowered the wheelchair user into the boat. I went onto the tail lift and the chap helping went into the boat to steady me down but on the way around he knocked my joystick which started the chair moving, luckily this one was prevented but wouldn't have ended well if I had gone over.

The lesson here was always slow the chair down and turn it off whilst on precarious tail lifts.

I did have one mishap a few years ago after attending the sand club in around November time it was dark and very cold.

My carer opened the van and chucked all her belongings into the front of the van including her jacket, phone and my car keys.

She got me into the van and clamped me down and shut the back door and the central locking on my van decided to lock itself locking myself and the keys inside the vehicle.

I was freezing as was she as her jacket was in the van with me. I felt so helpless and frustrated not being able to reach over and get the keys or unlock the door.

The only option was to smash a window which no one was able to do, we were in a car park so there wasn't anything hard around the people outside were trying bricks and everything. About 45 minutes later a fire engine turned up and smashed the passenger window with no problem.

The vehicle had never locked itself before and hasn't since.

It does always worry me though if I am inside the vehicle with the keys when someone goes to look at a parking meter for example.

I had an incident a few years ago which wasn't about me but about my manual wheelchair. Outside the house is where the tumble dryer is and where I keep my manual wheelchair. A carer went into the room and realised the wheelchair was gone.

I called the police and reported it stolen there wasn't anything they could do. Thankfully I always keep my power chair in doors.

The next day a carer went to walk around the local area to see if it could be found and he found it burnt out right next to the substation of all places.

Kids had obviously nicked it had some fun in it and then decided to set fire to it next to extremely powerful generators. The kids obviously didn't care about how important a wheelchair can be.

A couple of years ago we nipped into town in the van there were no disabled bays in the car park so my carer parked in a normal bay and went to get a ticket and left the radio on for me.

Literally 2 minutes had gone I saw a traffic warden skulking around the van, my van has a blue badge in the front and a blue wheelchair sticker on the back and I am 6ft 4 and my power chair is big.

He actually wrote a ticket whilst I was sat in the van. I was shouting my head off but he could not hear me or see me. My carer spotted this and ran back but the ticket had been written, he had a go at the traffic warden and then got me out the van so I could say my piece. I had no empathy for him but fancy giving a parking ticket to a guy in a wheelchair whilst he is in his van. The ticket was later dismissed after it was put in writing and explained.

Chapter 19

Chair problems

I have been pretty lucky regarding power chairs although things do go wrong.

My first power chair was on the NHS and had a rubbish battery and was always running out which meant it needed pushing.

I had one incident I can't remember the exact location it was some picturesque estate. I had gone with a group of friends thankfully! It was a wet rainy day we followed the sign for wheelchairs which went over a little bridge and the path started gradually going uphill and seemed to go around a hill.

After a few minutes there was a drop on one side which looked precarious so I turned around and headed back down which was lethal my friends had to stand on the right of the chair and push it and force it to stay on the path I had no control whatsoever and thought I was going over. If I would have been just with a carer this predicament would have been lethal, why there was a sign for wheelchair access I have no idea.

I had another bad access experience whilst in Norfolk visiting my father, we went around a lovely nature reserve which went through woods following wheelchair access signs and the path became narrower and narrower so the only way was forward and we came across a precarious looking bridge which was literally as wide as the chair with no safety rail. My father had to step into the marsh just to walk at the side of the chair just to keep it stable, my chair is very manoeuvrable but also very sensitive and it would have been very easy to come off.

I have got stuck in numerous garden centres due to the gravel, which is quite amusing but not the easiest thing to get out of.

It did this at one particular garden centre and the motor had blown on the chair so I had to be lifted into a manual chair taken home in the van and then my carer had to go back to pick up my power chair.

I also short-circuited the chair at an outdoor Travis concert in Sherwood forest it rained heavily when the concert finished, I'm sure they finished with why does it always rain on me. The chair had no power whatsoever, there is a mechanism at the back of the chair to make it manual although is very heavy, so I had to be pushed back to the van and then got stuck in the van at home as the chair would not move at all.

In summer 2007 I went to Leeds 02 festival there had been loads of rain and tickets were paid for and we were due to see Kaiser chiefs, the Twang, Pigeon detectives so we had to risk it.

We had no idea how bad the ground would be and it was very bad at one point going from one stage to another the mud was about a foot deep and very sloppy wet, most of the ground had plastic meshing over it and there was no way other than to go through it.

It took 4 people to help push the chair through the mud and the chair just went everywhere. I thought it was hilarious as people who were helping push couldn't get any traction and kept falling over in the mud. I was getting abuse and criticism for going through the mud; like I had any choice I certainly didn't expect it to be so deep.

Chapter 20

People's Attitude towards disability

In general I try to see the good in people although I have found across the years many people that are just so rude and arrogant in the way they talk to me just because I use a wheelchair.

I remember one time whilst still in hospital on one of my first few trips to Meadowhall I was still trying to acclimatise to my own world being in a wheelchair.

I was with nurses and managing okay, I had found some clothes I liked and wanted, which is actually quite a time-consuming exercise when you can't physically do things on your own and you are directing someone else.

The shop assistant was ever so patronising and asked the nurses if I was okay, and was happy to go ahead with the purchases. I replied something like I am here and if you are going to talk to people with me instead of myself then I will take my business elsewhere.

Which I did this was quite arduous having to find more clothes again but I felt really pleased with myself for not being talked down to. I thought the nurses were going to be mad at me for wasting their time. Their reaction was the opposite saying that I had probably learnt the biggest lesson yet, to take responsibility for myself and speak up myself and not let people just talk to my carers.

I find I get this a lot that people talk to the people that are with me instead of myself for example asking them; how is he? I have learnt to be more patient with my responses although if I'm in a bad mood I may snap.

I often find people shout at me; ARE YOU OK? I usually reply I am paralysed and not deaf. Why people assume they need to shout and think I am deaf just because I use a wheelchair is completely beyond me.

I also come across a lot of people who talk to me really slowly and assume because I use a wheelchair I must have learning problems or mental illness. Some people look astounded when I talk to them normally especially if I respond with; why do you assume I am simple just because I use a wheelchair, I have a degree for your information.

Then I get the other kind of people that are so rude in their approach and assume I'm going to tell a complete stranger why I am in a wheelchair when they blurt out something like; what's wrong with you? This happened the other day while sat in a pub enjoying a pint and listening to my brother's band.

I responded with; nothing, I'm just enjoying a pint and the music. She replied; but you're in a wheelchair so there must be something wrong with you. If people ask nicely and treat me with respect then I will answer with respect and explain a little of my condition.

I have also had people who I didn't know usually in pubs just come up to me and hit me on the leg and go; can you feel that? Which I can, I wouldn't go to an able-bodied person and run over their toes and then ask them if they can feel it so why do they feel its okay to do that?

A lot of people don't look down whilst going about their day-to-day business and don't acknowledge that there may be something happening below the line of sight.

I hate it when people just stop in front of me for what seems like no apparent reason and then give me a mouthful if I accidentally catch them. Admittedly sometimes I do that on purpose, if they were more aware of their surroundings and paying attention it wouldn't happen.

Normally I have a carer or someone with me but not all the time and I have had so many people go through a door and then not hold it open for me, so I have the door shut on me. This happens a lot in lifts, would it really hurt just to hold the door for 2 seconds.

Someone really pissed me of a few weeks ago. I was in a KFC that was pretty busy I went and found a table whilst my carer got the food some woman practically climbed over my legs and sat down at the table.

I did lose my temper with her and gave her a right mouthful for using me as a climbing frame. How rude and disrespectful is that!

One other thing I find quite a lot which I really hate is when people pat me on the head this is really frustrating I'm not a dog.

People's behaviour is often quite apparent to me due to studying counselling and being aware of people's body language, I quite often get a real patronising smile at people when they walk by or pass and I can tell they are trying to be sympathetic and thinking; you poor thing or something similar whether it's conscious or an unconscious the message is clear to me.

This chapter is only reflecting some negative attitudes towards disability. I have met and come across lots of very good people who have been helpful, non-judgemental, caring, considerate, and loyal and have made lots of friends who have had a positive influence on my life.

Part 5; Rolling back time

Chapter 21

Skating

I remember as a kid growing up in the 80s watching Back to the Future and thinking how cool Michael J Fox was on his skateboard so I wanted one.

I found one for sale in the local newspaper and could afford it due to having a paper round and working in the chicken farm , I don't remember how much I spent it was probably around £20.

My mum said it would be a waste of money and I will soon get bored of it like I did everything else as a kid. It turned out to be the best investment I ever had and helped me to find my character and personality.

It didn't come natural to me standing on a skateboard and it took months of practice to just stand and balance on it but it felt right.

My next door neighbour who was a couple of years younger than me bought one as he could see how much fun I was having so I always had someone to go out with.

Growing up in North Leverton there was plenty to explore and do but the main thing for me was the local Primary school which had benches, obstacles and a lovely smooth playground and was about a 10 minute push from home.

I spent hours down at the playground which eventually turned into years. I wouldn't go out without my board and would quite often skate to school.

On Sundays we would often get the bus into Retford and group up with various people from villages on the way and in the town soon realised there were more obstacles, steps, benches, slopes and flat land.

At a very young age I didn't realise in the town there was such a skating vibe and so many people enjoying the sport.

Through a friend of a friend I heard about the Hudson family who were all heavily involved in skateboarding or BMXing they had a massive vert ramp in their back garden and quite often at weekends there would be plenty of locals riding it and quite often professionals came down so it was great fun to watch and be involved in.

At the time one of the kids was sponsored by Vision street wear and the eldest brother was a photographer for the main skate magazines in the UK so it was always great ending up in a magazine albeit in the background and knowing people in photos.

I never got into vert skating properly the ramp was massive although not big enough for these boys as they ripped it down and built one higher and wider, it was great fun actually been involved in building the ramp.

It was mainly Saturdays where action took place as the town centre was open and busy so there was no way we could go street skating.

I used to enjoy going up and down the ramp and doing tricks about halfway up or on the flat but it was far too big and scary to me. I think it was about 10-12 foot high I did pad up once and dropped in on it and made it to the other side, it was hard enough running and climbing up it.

Eventually the town did get a purpose-built metal one about 6 feet high in the park which became a hangout.

In one of our local villages they had a wooden skateboard ramp which was dug into the ground but it was absolutely rubbish one side of the ramp had a curved transition and the other side was straight, even the vert boys couldn't do many tricks on it.

The council for our local village thought it was great and when we petitioned to have something made in North Leverton they made one even worse than the one at Rampton.

It was practically impossible to do any tricks on it was even difficult just getting one side to the other once it was built we had to be grateful for it. The best thing about it was that it was down at the bottom of a play park and was dug into the ground so no one could see what you were doing so it was a great place to have a smoke.

In the village I used to tip the metal goalpost up and drag it onto the smooth tennis court and use it as a sliding and grinding bar which was much more fun.

I was more into street skating especially flippy stuff and making the most of the urban terrain as were most of my friends. Before people were driving or if they were busy we would jump on a train to Doncaster, Sheffield or Nottingham , or we would go into various indoor skate parks around the country which was always great fun having access to quarter pipes, half pipes, fun boxes slide bars etc.

We would quite often go to Worksop and skate in the B&Q car park or the schools as there were some very good skaters whom a couple of which were professionals.

This was great as I could always get cheap boards and clothes.

I never liked school and the only time I ever put any effort in was if I was skating at the school.

I always took my board to college and used to go skating at dinner or would bunk off and go skating instead.

Figure 17;Me and my next door neighbor very young .

Figure 18;Skating in a suit .

Figure 19;Kick flip off a fly off in Leverton.

Chapter 22

Snow

I was never a fan of summer holidays unless they involved biking.

From about the age of nine the family always went skiing I always feel at peace in the mountains and have loved it from being a little boy, we had one family vacation in Florida every year we were dragged off skiing.

We started as a family langlaufing which is cross-country skiing I wasn't particularly taken by it, it was too slow and flat but my mother and father loved. It was nice seeing the scenery.

As kids myself and my brother joined kindergarten which are ski clubs for children where you learn the basics, we did this for a couple of years till we were confident and competent enough to go off together. I always remember my brother being faster than me.

My mother and father liked to take their time and dawdle down the mountain whereas my brother and I would come down as fast as possible. My father was and probably still is a casual skier, my mother's approach was even more casual she would go up the chair lifts and spend most of the day in the warmth of restaurants soaking up the scenery, reading and writing postcards and drinking hot chocolate and then gently ski down at the end of the day.

I think she liked the skiing experience but was just not too keen on the cold or the skiing bit, the actual skiing was more for the boys.

We were lucky that we got to go every year usually to Austria. After she died we didn't really go as a family again.

I got into snowboarding around the age of 21 starting off by going to Sheffield ski village which is a dry ski slope where we always used to go as kids usually for my brother's birthday which is bonfire night so it was always great fun skiing and looking out at the fireworks and bonfires.

My first proper winter snowboarding holiday was up in Aviemore in Scotland we drove up a few days before the New Year and my brother came up and met us there.

We stayed in a tee-pee. When we arrived at the campsite there was no snow so we put the tee-pee up and it snowed during the night at least a foot deep.

To say it was freezing was an understatement we had a tiny camping fire, the blanket we took with us literally froze solid we would wake up in the morning and gloves and boots were practically frozen.

It was great fun though especially tying a long piece of rope to the back of a van and being towed around the campfire on snowboards.

On the first day we weren't sure which lift passes to get so we bought one for the day and no one bothered checking them so we used the same pass all week.

I felt so alive on the snow it helped revitalise me and put the grief to one side.

The year after I went to a place we called the Valley in Klienwersatal in Austria the place was beautiful, and I was sick of life so saved up quit my job got myself a cheap B&B and stayed there for 4 weeks.

It was the most liberating freeing experience of my life, waking up every day to fresh snow, blue skies beautiful scenery and nothing to do but go boarding all day every day.

I learnt that if I was still with the same bunch of locals at the end of the day they would invite me around for the evening so I would have company, food drink and smoke (I did contribute financially to this) so I learnt the only way to ride was to ride fast.

I really enjoyed the trick side of snowboarding especially going off jumps and landing in deep snow but for me snowboarding was more about being at one with the environment. There is no other feeling than the freedom of carving through deep snow it's like walking on air.

I am a sucker for scenery and when in the mountains I would look into the horizon and it was often difficult to figure out where the earth stopped and the heavens started.

I went back the year after with different friends and we stayed in someone's basement, which no one was impressed with but it was free.

I kept my snowboard it is the one thing that I wasn't prepared to sell or give away as it held too many memories and is the only physical item I hung onto. I decided to make it into a shelf in my bedroom. When I bought the board it probably retailed at about 400 quid so it's an expensive shelf but I am so glad I kept it.

Figure 20;Me mum and my brother on our first skiing trip.

Figure 21;Camping in a teepee in Aviemore.

Figure 22;Brrr inside the teepee with just a tiny heater.

Figure 23;My brother,Jamie,Jeff and me in Aviemore.

Figure 24;Me and my board in Aviemore.

Figure 25;Tweaking a grab in Austria.

Figure 26;Getting high.

Figure 27;Nice air.

Chapter 23

Bikes

Bikes were a massive part of my life due to not driving a car I had to rely on myself and my pushbike to get from A to B.

This was always frustrating and enjoyable at the same time as most of my life I spent Living in North Leverton and the nearest town was 5 miles away which was quite a hilly journey.

Leverton hill is quite steep and long. Going down it was always great fun, getting back a bit after a day's work was quite challenging.

The longest ride I had was about 15 miles which was quite a trek. Not driving often came up in job interviews and they would worry whether or not I would be reliable which I was most of the time. Sometimes I hated not driving especially when the weather was bad it was horrible getting drenched and cold before turning up at work especially if I didn't have a change of clothes, also getting sweaty before work.

I loved biking for pleasure and had really good friends who were into mountain biking we travelled all around the country at weekends which usually involved camping we went to the Lake District, Peak District, Scotland and Wales.

Sometimes we would just be going off-road and sometimes we knew we were going for a reason because the mountain routes were the best in the country with extremely fast downhill's and long slow grinding up hills. Most of the time we would be out on the bikes for the full day.

My favourite route was in Scotland called the devil's staircase and it went on for miles.

Biking wasn't always about challenging, adrenaline, excitement; it was always about fun and enjoying the environment and surroundings.

It was quite often we would get to the top of the mountain and it would be time for a joint or 2, some of the lads didn't smoke and thought it was pretty crazy and defeating the object of being out in the fresh air exercising. For us it was a way of life.

In hindsight it was pretty daft getting stoned before attempting some of the trickiest fastest mountains in the country.

If we were just cross-countrying and on pleasure rides there was always time to sit and skin up. Some rides involved stopping pub to pub. For me this was worse drinking 4 or 5 pints is not the wisest thing to do.

I always remember one particular bike ride I ended up with punctures and after about 5 pints it seemed like a good idea to travel on the back of my mate's bike with my bike on my shoulder, we were all over the road it was funny though.

I always loved thursday nights, a lot of us would group up and ride up to Clumber park come rain or shine and race around the woods, and this would be especially fun in winter as everyone had really powerful spotlights on their bikes.

My mates are still involved they go to France every year on the downhill bikes and ride down the ski runs. Early on my mates felt awkward talking about biking holidays but I am always keen to hear where they go, who went the fastest and who came off the most.

At times I actually hated being on a bike open to the elements but when this part of my life was taken away from me it was so hard coming to terms with something you take for granted and then aren't able to do any more.

I have spent so much time whilst able-bodied with wheels under me that Life Rolls On has been appropriate to me for a long time.

Figure 28;Even as a kid my bike was my favourite toy.

Figure 29;Mountain biking in Wales.

Figure 30;Mountain biking in Scotland.

Figure 31;Devils staircase in Scotland come rain or shine.

Figure 32;About to crash my front wheel is balanced on a rock.

Chapter 24

Reflections and the impact of losing my mother

I remember the day when my dad came home and walked in crying, he turned the TV off and said "I don't know how to tell you both but your mother has died."

I was only 18 and she was in her early 40s.

There had been no indication to me she had been ill and had been suffering and it came completely out of the blue.

For a couple of weeks she hadn't seemed herself, one night we heard her crying out

"Why me? " - she was a deeply religious person. I think she knew she was ill but didn't tell anyone and was crying out to Jesus. She went into hospital and never came back.

There are four phases of adult mourning, the first of which being shock and numbness, the second being anger, guilt and rejection, the third being depression and final stage is seen as where life continues.

Initially all I could feel was shock and numbness; due to the fact I didn't know anything was wrong.

I remember at the funeral, the director said to me "if you can cope with this, you can cope with anything life will throw at you."

Initially this ripped our family apart. My dad gave up work and went to do a boat building course in Norfolk, where he met his new partner.

My brother went to university and I stayed at the family home, and dad came home at weekends, and I would vanish for the weekend.

At this stage I definitely felt guilty and angry for not knowing she wasn't we. If I'd been a good son surely she would have been able to tell me she was ill, I also felt rejection as I was left in the family home with no support.

I knew life would go on but had no idea how difficult it would make school life as I was doing my A-levels, although I had no interest and failed these and dropped out of school.

I found maintaining relationships throughout the years has always been difficult; I always seemed to be doing my own thing and drove people away.

I found getting close to people extremely difficult, and I tended to avoid getting too involved in order to evade the hurt and pain that went with rejection.

This would tie in with the depression stage of mourning, lack of self-esteem, confidence, and self-worth.

I have internalised her and feel she has been watching out for me throughout my life.

People often say I look like her, which I draw great comfort from.

I came to the conclusion life is short and to try and get as much enjoyment as possible out of what I do enjoy and try various activities and see different parts of the world.

This is the stage of accepting the loss and life goes on.

It is important to grieve the loss of a loved one and face reality in order to move forward.

Without going through some kind of process moving on may become difficult.

My mother was kind, caring, patient and a good listener, which I feel are traits I have inherited, and become my personal moral qualities, which have enabled me to follow my life's path and become a counsellor.

My dad is more of a 'hands-on', 'fix-it' kind of guy.
Initially it took a few years for me to go down to the grave and pay my respects, now I go quite often and tell her what I have been doing, and who I am helping through counselling.

I have tattooed on my ankle the day she was born and the day she died as a permanent reminder.

I do believe life goes on after death, and I will see her again.

Since having a life changing injury I had my own spiritual awakening. I am a believer that things happen for a reason and when my time is up I hope my consciousness will leave my body the way a butterfly leaves its cocoon and become part of the whole of global consciousness. I am now 37 and not a day goes by when my mother isn't in my heart.

Figure 33;One of my favourites of my mum.

Chapter 25

Fun down at Sundown

During the summer of 98 I got a job working at a local fun park for children called Sundown Adventure land.

The park was about a 15 minute bike ride from where I used to live and quite often there would be other people going at the same time so we could ride up together.

The job was mainly as ride operatives and offering assistance around the park including cleaning up and maintenance, the hours were 11 until 5.

I use the term job very loosely. I had to drive a train around the same track endless times and the train was automated so all I had to do was get people on drive round the track and press a few buttons to operate the commentary, not many people have train driver on their

CV. I can still remember most of the dialogue from that train.

I also had to operate Santa's sleigh ride in a dark environment with Jingle Bells playing constantly which drove you mental especially in summer.

The other ride was a pirate boat ride. In peak season workers had to dress up either as a pirate, Santa's helpers or a cowboy train driver.

It was very boring monotonous repetitive work getting people on and off rides so we would amuse ourselves by mucking around with kids and by stomping and making noise depending on how attractive women on the ride were, if it was a loud stomp workers at the other end would know to look out for someone attractive.

In peak summer myself and a friend actually got told off by management for having too much fun we were dressed as pirates and shooting kids with water pistols which they loved, surely in the job description having fun with kids was part of the criteria but apparently not.

The entrance to the boat ride was like a shack where people queued up, at one end in the middle was a large conveyor belt which was sloped on one end so the barrels which were about 6 foot diameter and 3 foot deep would rise up out of the water. They would then rise onto the conveyor belt where we would assist people getting on and off and then the barrel would drop off into the water and go around the ride.

I was working on it on my own one-day I had stopped the belt to help someone on and noticed an empty barrel come up the slope and stopped and then another one came up and stopped and was at a steep angle, I remember panicking thinking that I had to get the ride moving again as more boats were coming around when I saw another barrel coming around the corner with an old lady and her grandkids either side of her so all the weight was on one side, I saw the barrel flip over and land on top of the lady and 2 kids. I didn't have time to think I just jumped straight towards the water which was murky and about 4 foot deep somehow I managed to get the boat out of the water which usually took 2 people and got the kids out of the water and got the old lady out.

They were terrified and I had to send them to the nearest restaurant on their own and ask for help and first aid as the ride was still going and I had boats going around.

I was dripping wet in a pirate costume in a complete state and it was about half an hour before any staff members actually came to relieve me and see if I was all right.

I believe the lady sued the fun park and the health and safety changed so 2 people were on the ride at all times.

I feel this is one of my proudest moments thankfully they were okay, having a child drown whilst working as a pirate is not something I want on my conscience. Who knows how other people would have reacted in that situation

Chapter 26

Work

I had the mentality of working to live not living to work. My first job was while I was at school at a local chicken farm in the morning and after school we would go and collect the eggs.

I would also have to feed the chickens and on a weekend we would have to grade the eggs, which meant either placing eggs on a conveyor belt for hours on one end or sitting inside a dark room where the eggs went over light and you had to pull-out cracked ones or you were at the end of the machine putting the eggs in trays or boxes.

The chicken farm owner was great and gave a lot of young people in the village an opportunity to earn some money.

After leaving school with not many qualifications I was at Netto stacking shelves, rotating stock, filling freezers and generally being a dogsbody. The people I worked with were great and we always had a laugh which we needed to have as the job was awful.

While on the early shift I had to be a work at 5 AM in order to offload trucks and get the supermarket ready for the day. Due to the fact I never drove I had to rely on myself and my push-bike.

At the time I lived in North Leverton and worked in Retford so had a 5 mile bike ride first and had to be up at 4 AM and was paid 2 pounds an hour for the privilege and treated like dirt most of the time. If I was on an early shift I would try and stay at a mate's house which usually meant we got off our heads the night before.

I stuck it out around 8 months.

I then got a job with a printing firm called Rainbow copy shop I'm not entirely sure how I got this job as I had no experience working in printers.

I got trained up and shown how to use the guillotine as my main duty was trimming the edges off letter heads, compliment slips, cutting down business cards and leaflets and flyers. I was known as a print finisher i.e. once the finished product had been printed it was my responsibility to get the product out and boxed up. I also had to make receipt pads and books and mix the ink and prepare the paper in order to keep the printer printing.

A lot of the work was fiddly and relied on hand eye coordination and was mainly work with my hands.

The office was in town and we were a couple of miles away working in a small group which was good as I never really saw the boss who I never got on with his name was Todd and we called him the Todd father as he was strict.

I seem to remember him pissing me off one day and he accused me of not doing something even though I showed him the work and he stressed out on me so I walked out.

The company became massive and is now a multi-million pound company it's one of those fork in the road moments whereas had I not walked out of my job my life may have gone in a different direction and I probably would've had a career for life. I now live just around the corner from the complex which is ironic.

I found out after I left he had 3 people doing what I was doing myself. I worked there for around 18 months.

I then got a real soul sapping job in a shed factory rolling up felt for sheds which was quite a trek from where I lived and had a 15 mile bike ride to and from work. Sometimes I could get a lift which I was always grateful for as I knew a few people who worked there and we would often rotate between ourselves different jobs just to alleviate the boredom so some days I would be counting out nails for the shed kits or painting the timber with spray. I was meant to be rolling felt for the roofs. It was all very mind numbing and boring and monotonous.

I managed to stick this out for about 6 months as it was good money.

My working career really took a slump when I got a job in a chicken factory called J Jollies in Gainsborough and believe me there was nothing jolly about the place. I got dumped on the production line and my duties were pick the chicken up stick Chicken on a rotating spike, Pick the chicken up stick Chicken on a rotating spike and repeat for 10 hours. Mind-numbing, soul destroying, frustrating, boring doesn't even come close; there were people there who had been doing the same job day in day out for 10 years the chickens had higher Iqs and they were dead.

I was given a locker without a door so each morning I had to find and steal other people's hats or wellies I survived here about 2 weeks.

I then got a job at Sundown Adventure land as a ride attendant and park cleaner and worked there about 6 months as discussed in a previous chapter.

I then got a job at a local paper mill where they made wallpaper which actually paid really well. I worked here for about 6 months and saved up and went to Austria for a month.

It was another boring repetitive monotonous job all done by machines. I rolled a roll of wallpaper on the machine and then put it in a box and then I rolled a roll of wallpaper on the machine and then put it in a box and repeat. Some days I would swap machines with others and be on a wrapping machine so instead of rolling I would be wrapping and boxing admittedly it was really slack and very easy work and very well paid.

After coming back from Austria I got another job in a printing factory called Acorn Maltone as a print finisher again mainly operating a guillotine. I really enjoyed working in printers although a lot of the tasks were repetitive there were always different jobs that needed doing whether it was guillotining, mixing or cutting paper, I absolutely loved working on a guillotine which was state-of-the-art fully computerised and I would start with a massive sheet of A2 and end up hopefully with 50 or so stacks of business cards.

It was always tricky work and quite easy to make a mistake by turning paper the wrong way and cutting straight through the text, which would mean the whole job would have to be reprinted. I worked here for about 2 years up to my injury; ironically my brother took over my job after my injury.

Escaping and getting out of the rat race of work has been positive outcome although I wish it would have been under different circumstances my time became my own.

Chapter 27

Tattoos

I've always been a fan of tattoos. I had my first one done while down in Newquay in 95. I had it done on my left arm it is a black tribal band. I was off my head at the time which is never recommended. I always liked the actual design but the person who did it was rubbish, it wasn't quite symmetrical and the black ink wasn't the same all the way through, after a couple of years I eventually decided to get it tidied up. Initially the tattoo artist laughed at it and he had to spend an hour working on the outline just to tidy up before he could start actually extending it. He did a really good job and it looks good now. It doesn't really have much meaning it is just a design I see it as representative of the darkness I went through losing my mother.

My mate who also had his done at the same time went to the same guy and had his fixed up as his originally looked awful too.

I have on my left ankle my mother's date of birth and the day she died in the same font as the grave, which is a nice personal reminder.

I always wanted my back doing while into my skateboarding and snowboarding so I opted for some nice Celtic knot work. Which is meant to symbolise Infinity as there is no start and no end, I then added 2 Celtic dogs which symbolised power which mix into 2 Celtic birds which symbolise freedom.

I feel it's a good visual representation of how I chose to live my life and I draw strength from the symbolism, although I never quite got it finished to how I wanted it.

These 3 were done before my injury and are reflective of my life.

Whilst in hospital people would often comment on them, some people would ask if I regret having them done and the answer is always no they are part of me and a permanent reminder and the only real part of my body that didn't change after injury.

I was always keen to have more and spoke to doctors and other people who have had spinal injury and had tattoos. The doctor's opinion was wait a few years till your body is completely settled down and if I do have more have them where my body is less affected from a spinal injury i.e. the arms, a lot of people said they love having tattoos done after paralysis as the pain is nowhere near how it used to be and a lot of people say they can't even feel it being done now. Use common sense if thinking of getting a tattoo they are there for forever their great value for money if you ask me. Nothing else lasts forever.

I always wanted my right arm doing and was never sure what to do with it and was not sure how my body would react.

I decided around 2007 to finally do it. I explained to the guy my concern but also what I wanted. I said I wanted something full-colour and all natural and reflected the change I had been through. I remember him saying here's another nutter with grand idea who isn't going to follow through; I think I replied once I commit to something I see it through.

I was pretty sure my body would be okay and I would be able to tolerate pain the only way to find out was to get on with it, frankly It wasn't too bad. I ended up with a water lily with a butterfly on, with a dragonfly flying above, a coi fish swimming underneath the water with mountains and the sun in the background.

After a couple of years I decided to get one on my shin of a Tiger as I love the creatures as they are strong and independent and also quite solitary. It wasn't too bad at all having my leg done although it was very tender and sore the third hour.

My father hated me having them done but it is my body and gives me something to like about it.

Figure 34;Black tribal.

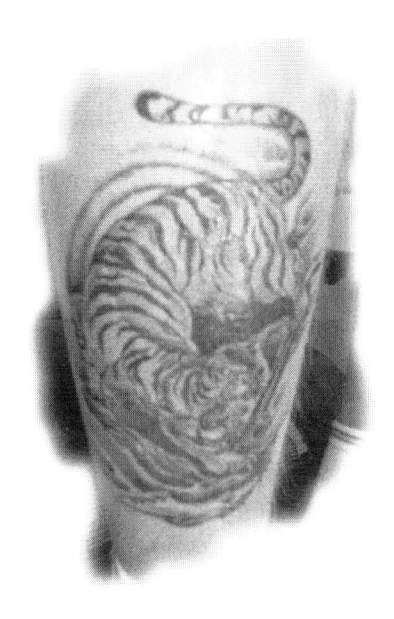

Figure 35;Tiger.

Figure 36;Peaceful place .

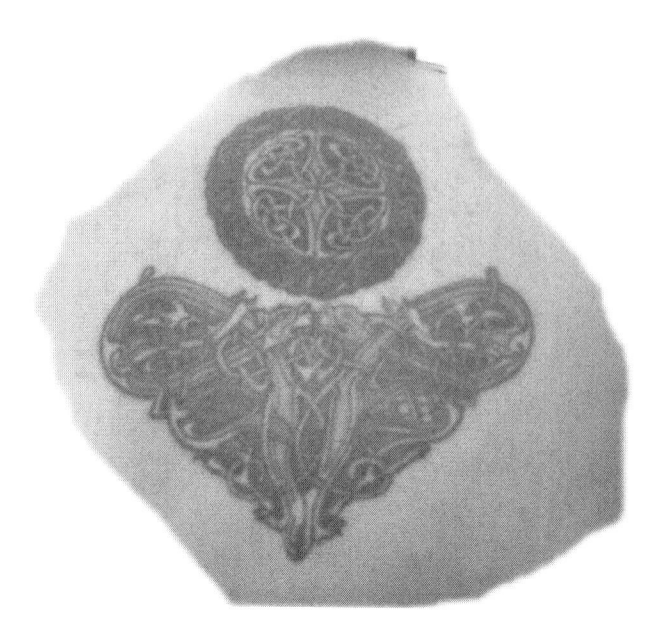

Figure 37;Celtic knot work.

Part 6; Rolling up towards a degree

Chapter 28

Starting college

I spent a lot of time through 2000 and the start of 2001 sorting out practical issues whilst thinking and wondering what I was now going to do with the rest of my life.

I was always sporting whilst able-bodied although not into your typical sports I loved playing basketball but was more into skateboarding, snowboarding and mountain biking.

I knew I wanted to do something involving sports but wasn't sure what.

I arranged an interview at North Nott's College I discussed with academic support my practical needs and it sounded promising about getting a note taker, which would help with typing and paperwork.

I met Dave in 2001 he was a sports tutor he had never worked with a wheelchair user in sports let alone such a high level of physical disability.

I owe a great deal to Dave and we became good friends he was the first person to give me a chance and an opportunity and helped me find myself and start a road to recovery.

We talked about a level 1 sports award called the community sports leader award. Neither of us knew how I would be able to get through the course as it had physical requirements, he seemed determined as I was to give it a go and learn as we went along.

Having someone take notes about lessons was a great help and it meant I could concentrate and focus on the lesson.

I wasn't particularly academic and never really cared about school or education at the time, I did have 4 GCSEs at C or above. I did start my A-levels at the time my mother passed away so doing A-levels seemed irrelevant.

One of my biggest fears for starting the course was knowing that I will have to do 10 hours coaching in the community which terrified me.

I couldn't get involved physically in sessions until we got more confident and aware of how to adapt. Verbally I was fine I used either the tutor or students to help physically do demonstrations and help with equipment.

I learnt to be more vocal and directive describing what I wanted for the sessions and had to describe warm-ups, session content, skills and cool downs.

My note taker helped me to do session plans. Other than being physically disabled and relying on a power chair I had real problems projecting my voice in sports halls as I got out of breath very quickly and tired very quickly, I did get better at projecting my voice and strapped a whistle to my hand which helped silence everyone before I could talk.

I learned a lot about positioning myself so I was talking directly to a group or individual and found I had to move around a lot.

One game I was particularly good at directing and refereeing was boccia. (More on later)

I heard about a club that ran in Retford called the SAND club which stands for see the ability not the disability and I felt this would be ideal for my placement.

When I met with the organizers and explained what I was studying they were keen to give me a go.

I was really keen to work with people and children with disabilities I felt I would be able to empathise with them and them me.

I completed my 10 voluntary hours with the club and had to write up my progress, session plans and how I had been involved etc. I enjoyed these 10 hours that much 10 years later I'm still heavily involved in the club (more on the club later.)

I successfully passed the Csla course.

I heard about a group based in Nottingham called sports direct that offered coaching courses for people with disabilities and also ran sessions for people with disabilities.

I signed up for as many courses as possible and after a while I had level 2 qualifications in Boccia, table top games, zone hockey, first aid, working with people with disabilities, wheelchair basketball to name a few.

I became quite confident and competent at delivering sports sessions and really enjoyed the challenge.

The people from the Sand sports club recognised the hard work and effort I was putting in and nominated me in 2002 for the Bassetlaw sports awards in a category called achievement in disability sport.

I was very pleased the hard work had been noticed I didn't think I would win so was very happy when I did win the award, I was also nominated in another category without my knowledge this category was achievement through adversity which I also won so ended up coming away with 2 trophies and feeling very pleased with my progress.

I won the achievement in disability sport award again in 2009.

I advanced my education at college by continuing studying sports science and did specific modules based around coaching, nutrition and physiology. For this placement I chose to work in a different field and successfully completed 10 coaching sessions with able-bodied primary school children, which worked out well as I had a fellow student with me who wasn't very communicative so I did the talking and directing and he helped with the equipment and demonstrations etc.

One of the hardest things about working with such young children was dealing with their curiosity about me being a wheelchair user, knowing how to explain and what to tell them can be difficult I find breaking it down and explaining in simple terms is the best approach.

I once got asked by a child; what's it like being a king? Having everything done for you and sitting on your throne. I see his logic but a strange question to answer.

In about 2003-2004 I was quite qualified as a sports coach; I never considered taking it further especially not to degree level.

Figure 38;Me and Dave at North Notts community arena.

Chapter 29

Boccia

Boccia is a game specifically aimed at people with disabilities.

One team plays against another, usually 3 people per team. Each team has 6 balls either red or blue; a white Jack ball is thrown into the court which is about the size of a badminton court.

The team who is furthest away from the white plays.

The team at the end of each game with most balls nearest to the white wins points, 6 games are played the team with the most points wins.

Boccia can be played by any person with any ability the ball can be thrown, rolled, kicked or rolled down a ramp or chute.

Boccia interested me from the very start the only equipment are balls and a court and once they have been thrown and the game is over I get the participants to pick up their own balls.

Once I knew how the game was played I was very capable of delivering, coaching or refereeing the game.

I have played Boccia with every age group possible from young children, to young adults, to grown-ups and with the elderly, and a wide range of abilities and disabilities due to the simple yet competitive nature of the game people always have fun playing the game and take it very seriously and get very competitive.

I have refereed at local competition level and refereed at Nott's youth games at national level.

I have been involved in many leagues throughout the years and still enjoy the game, sometimes I do get to play using a ramp to propel the ball I do enjoy playing but rather prefer being the coach or referee especially when it's a final or an important match.

Chapter 30

The SAND club

I got involved with the SAND sports club in 2001 as part of the community sports leader award. SAND stands for see the ability not the disability.

At the time I just wanted to complete 10 voluntary hours in order to get a qualification. I had no idea the impact the club would have on me and vice versa.

I first met Sian who was one of the people that ran it and they were keen to give me a go; when I started I think there were maybe 10 members ranging from all kinds of disabilities. Now the club has a lot more members and offers trial events and sports for a wide number due to a festival we run each year. I think there are between 40-50 people on the books now.

Initially I only observed children's behaviour and the coach's approach and I interacted with the members.

I ran warm-ups at first and as my confidence grew the more they let me lead and practice. At first the club was in a small hall so it was easy projecting my voice we later moved to a bigger venue and then a bigger one still.

The club now runs every Monday night in term time at Worksop College from 6 o'clock to 7 o'clock, and swimming is on a Thursday night at Bircotes Leisure Centre.

At one point we were running the club twice a week at 2 different venues but one had to go for financial reasons as the club isn't funded.

The sand club gave me an opportunity to work more with disabled children and practice running sports sessions and improve my confidence.

I found ways of adapting my coaching style and how to adapt many sports and games for different abilities, we often have students on various sports courses helping and participating in the club which helps them learn to adapt and we have to evaluate their session plans and coaching.

At the club we promote independence and to look beyond just the sporting element by watching how the children interact and build their own social and personal skills.

We don't focus on one particular sport we encourage different coaches to come in and teach.

Over the years we have introduced many different sports for children to try including all generic sports football, basketball, cricket and tennis etc.

We have also tried tai chi, ken do, archery, boxercice and dancing and cheer leading.

Within the club there is a real sense of family and everyone is accepting and understanding about each disability.

We have also introduced activity weekends which for a lot of the children have been the first time away from parents.

Last year the club went to the Lake District where myself and the children went canoeing, abseiling and looking around mines.

Myself I conquered one of my biggest demons and participated in a wheelchair abseil which helped me face my fears.

One of my fondest memories which I will always cherish came from this weekend seeing our ill-est, most vulnerable and most disabled child 20 foot up a climbing wall.

Another one was on the last afternoon before leaving. Myself and a volunteer and a wheelchair user were sat talking when he said how good the weekend was and how he had realized that he can experience different activities and how he should and could do more for himself and should not be scared any more just because he needs a wheelchair.

It was very touching.

Every year we also arrange to go to a pantomime which is for the kids, honest! Oh no it's not Oh yes it is.

We also do regular fund raising for the club. Recently we offered a bag packing service at Tesco's which was great seeing how the members interacted with the general public and vice versa.

We had a family member organize a kid's party and bbq with face painting etc. We also had a volunteer's brother in law who is a house / indie DJ give up his time and do a gig which was so successful he has agreed to do it again along with 2 other bands to help keep the club running.

I have been involved with the club for over 10 years now and am still coming up with challenging interesting ideas to help the children improve hand eye coordination and social skills.

The children see that I am not going to be beaten by my disability therefore they become more accepting of themselves. The feeling of satisfaction and worth watching and seeing how the children develop over time is extremely satisfying as they get older and get involved in college and higher education.

Figure 39;SAND sports club as part of the Bassetlaw games.

Figure 40;Hanging around in the Lake District.

Figure 41;Wheelchair absailing.

Chapter 31

Sport relief mile 2012

I decided to do the sports relief mile the day before the event and it was local in the nearby park. I wanted to do it as a challenge and to raise some money.

Just because I use a power chair there is no reason not to participate in a social fund-raising event. It was over grass which was very wet and slippy which made the chair quite tricky to control as the terrain was rough and I got bounced about a fair bit also there were some quite steep sections which I didn't think there would be, at one point the chair did struggle and my carer had to give me a push.

It was nice getting some positive feedback and encouragement from the walkers and runners.

It really tested the chair and it coped okay with it at one point my carer did say she was a bit worried about it taking over some of the downhill's as the chair does have a tendency to tip forward whilst going downhill, when I stop the chair does tip forward which can quite worrying at times but I do have faith in the chair. I raised 30 pounds. Entrance fee of 6 pounds so it all helps.

The important thing to me is breaking down the barriers and just because I use a wheelchair there is no reason I should not be able to join in, but it also sends a positive message to members of our local disabled sports club.

Figure 42;Sport relief mile 2012.

Chapter 32

Inclusive sports project

In around 2005 the tutor who I'd worked with previously at college got back into touch with me saying he wanted to run more sessions for the learning development and physical needs students at college.

I saw this is a great opportunity to start working with younger adults with physical or cognitive processing problems this presented a new challenge of working with different people and with them being older we were more able to concentrate on actual sports and competitive games instead of more fun orientated games.

It was great working with him again and seeing how his attitude and approach to working with disability had changed and altered so much since initially meeting me in 2001. He was really promoting inclusive sport to the college and breaking down barriers within the college and other colleges and over the years we got 2 other colleges involved in friendly competition with our students in football, boccia and new age curling which I have been involved in refereeing.

I also helped teach the CSLA course which I initially started out on to a group of young adults with physical or learning difficulties which was very rewarding seeing other students gain a qualification and it showed how myself and Dave had grown and how we were able to cope with delivering the course and how we had ironed out all the obstacles and barriers which we had come across whilst I was getting through the same course.

Working for the college gave me a real sense of achievement and self-worth. I actually gained financial reward for doing the coaching which was a great feeling of worth being able to earn a bit more money for myself although in the end this caused too many problems with me earning a small amount of money with the nice people at the benefits office, which was ridiculous. I am only allowed to earn £20 a week and the college were paying me £19 an hour and the sessions were one and a half hours so about £30 per session per week anything over the allocated allowance was taken off me. This became a real hindrance and flaw for me and my benefits.

The confidence, self-worth and independence that came from doing something productive and helpful towards others should have some financial gain.

There is no financial incentive for people with disabilities on benefits to try and earn a few extra quid and I can see why a lot of people don't bother there is only so much of one's time that can be given voluntarily especially occurring travelling costs with diesel etc.

Chapter 33

Teacher training

Sports' coaching was going very well and I was getting a lot out of it, I really enjoyed the challenge of teaching the community sports leader award and thought this is the direction I wanted to go in.

I looked into courses the college offered and signed up for an introduction to teaching, I think it was a 10 week course I didn't particularly like the tutor but I did learn a lot about presenting and how to use PowerPoint which has been extremely helpful.

I decided I liked the teaching of sports coaching but only in sports halls and decided I didn't want to be stuck teaching in classrooms. I came to the decision not to pursue this field of study I wanted to be able to help people and didn't think teaching was the right direction for me so thought long and hard about which new direction would utilise the ability that I have and to be able to help people so I started studying counselling.

Chapter 34

Counselling; college

Around 2005 after deciding that teacher training wasn't for me I felt I had more to offer than just working in sports and wanted to be able to help people in a different way and I felt I was strong enough to be able to offer more of myself although I still had lots of my own questions and conflicting internal dialogue.

I had no idea what counselling involved and there would be so many different theoretical viewpoints, I thought it was mainly about giving advice to others this was an opinion which soon changed.

I studied at North Nott's college part-time for 4 years during this time we looked at most of the major contributors and different aspects of theory ranging from Carl Rogers and Person centred theory; Arron

Beck with cognitive behaviour therapy but the last 2 years we concentrated and focused on psycho-dynamic theory which is the work of Freud, Jung, Winnicot, Klein and Erickson. I have no intention of boring people with theory.

I found psycho-dynamic theory extremely interesting and powerful as it mainly dealt with looking at the unconscious mind and defence mechanisms which are in place, and the impact of childhood or the past on the present.

I learnt a lot about my own mind and the internal processes which have been going on.

The main difference in starting studying counselling was the age group and gender, while studying sports and related topics groups mainly consisted of 18 to 20-year-olds most of which had no interest in studying.

The counselling group mainly consisted of women in their 30s and 40s who actually wanted to improve their education, interestingly the group was mainly female but the tutor was male.

Whilst at college I had to do all kinds of presentations and discussions ranging from Freud's structure of personality, how to offer counselling to somebody wanting a sex change and how to set up and start your own counselling practice.

In college we ran through different scenarios involving role-playing as we were told not to use our own personal stuff.

We often practised in trios for around 15 minutes with one person being the counsellor one person being the client and the third observing the Counsellor and giving feedback on what they had heard and seen the counsellor say, how they had introduced themselves, how they had set boundaries, any evidence of putting theory into practice.

I always remember how safe the practice sessions felt and it was okay if I said the wrong thing or didn't know how to handle something.

On the last year of the course we had to work with real clients and complete 50 hours one-on-one with clients and 10 hours of supervision.

I struggled to find a placement and eventually I contacted Eastgate resource centre which is a day centre mainly for people with disabilities, they didn't have a counselling service in place although there was a chap who was very helpful and wanted to set one up which also helped with what he was studying.

Not having anything set in place made it scarier but it was also good starting from scratch.

I will never forget my first session with a real client with emotional problems. I introduced myself and explained about confidentiality and boundaries and tried to remember everything I had learned and practised, I had the angriest person I've ever met and for about half an hour he pretty much was shouting at me and then stormed off. I was pretty scared I would get hit and wondered what I had let myself in for. The reality of working with real people with real issues hit home.

I completed my 50 hours with no more incidents and got to work with a wide range of problems and disabilities.

I had the same tutor for the 4 years and got to know how he wanted essays to be written so did well and got good marks. I had a real good understanding of the psycho-dynamic approach and people would ask for me to be able to explain things.

The course ended with a written exam explaining how psycho-dynamic theory had been beneficial to working with clients, I had to have my own individual room I dictated and had someone write for me, poor lass ended up writing 16 pages of A4.

I found it very strange having somebody else write for me it was hard going at a slower pace and making sure she had written what I had said before I moved on to the next sentence. I would forget my train of thought as I had to keep repeating myself, whereas talking to a computer for dictating I can go at my own pace and the computer keeps up, Dragon is very accurate although every now and again it comes up with random words.

In 2009 I gained my higher diploma in counselling. I was surprised I had a graduation ceremony at college and got to where the full cap and gown unfortunately my father and his partner weren't able to attend the ceremony but my brother did.

I felt really pleased with myself for completing the course and heard that I would now be able to jump on the last year of a degree course.

Chapter 35

Counselling; Degree course

I applied to the University of Nottingham and was offered an interview.

I was terrified for this interview and wasn't feeling very well; thankfully my interview was mainly a one-on-one chat for an hour or so. I felt it went very well and I had presented myself as best I could and the course leader was keen to read some of my existing work and he said I would be better applying for a part-time course which would make funding easier and also give me more time to complete the work load and would take about 14 months not 6 if I did it full-time.

I seem to think he offered me a place after a couple of days. I was ecstatic at the thought of going on to a degree even if it was from a different theoretical perspective.

I chose the modules I wanted to take and I chose comparative humanistic counselling; where I got to look at different humanistic theories. I felt fairly confident with the first piece of written work although I had not written anything for a year or so.

Writing to the level required was extremely difficult as I had to write from different perspectives and from a different theory.

I did get some positive feedback for this essay but picked up lots of criticism so I realised I had to learn how to restructure essays, how to do proper referencing and how to write at a high level.

The other modules I chose were working with trauma, working with grief and loss and working with addiction.

Each essay was marked by a different tutor and all were looking for something different.

I felt an outsider at first as most of the group had been working together for a couple of years, the group were really friendly and helpful and I soon felt part of the team and I got some good advice on essay writing.

We met up at the group every month and had a group process session which was great and helped me understand the person centred theory more.

I had to complete 100 hours of counselling and 25 hours of supervision. I did my placement for a charity called Adept which mainly promoted abstinence from alcohol and drugs.

I did my placement at a local medical centre in Worksop. I really enjoyed the challenge of working with such a wide range of conditions ranging from depression, addiction, illness, disability, social anxiety, trauma and loss.

My supervision was fort nightly in Nottingham and was inside the only building I have ever come across I could not access easily. There were 3 steps outside the building so I had to go in my manual wheelchair and be physically lifted up the steps. I am grateful to everyone who persevered with this. I hated it, not only the danger to me but I didn't want to be responsible for hurting some ones back.

I even worked with a deaf client which presented a huge amount of problems as although he could lip read he didn't get a great deal from my body language. We did have an interpreter in sessions who was made aware of confidentiality.

It was the first time I had really spoken to somebody who's completely deaf let alone offered counselling, To me it was another way of breaking down barriers and although we had completely different disabilities we could empathise with each other.

I personally would like to have spent a lot more time working with this client as I started to learn some of the signs instead of having to rely on the interpreter but after 6 sessions only he didn't want to pursue it in more

I wanted to broaden my horizons and really feel I worked with a wide range and scope of problems.

I had counselling myself throughout the year and it really helped me get through the year and deal with lots of issues. I developed a greater understanding of myself and what I had been through and how much growth I have experienced, it helped me clarify certain chapters of my life and helped me put a lot of the pieces together I certainly wouldn't have been able to write this beforehand.

I think my essay writing came on in leaps and bounds I got good marks for 3 of the essays and the other 3 not so good, I wanted to come out with a 2; 1.

I ended up with a 2; 2 which I found disappointing after all the hard work I had put in and it took me a while to be happy with the fact that I had gotten a degree.

For me the essay writing and the academic side of gaining a degree although extremely important in how you are assessed and judged on your practice it is not the most important part. The emotional and personal growth I experienced throughout the year are much more important.

The work that I did with clients was the most positive satisfying element; I gained a deeper understanding of the human condition from working with clients.

I learned a different theoretical background; I became much more confident in my own ability and approach to Counselling. I became more confident in establishing boundaries and maintaining a contract, I developed a less judgemental attitude, I became more confident in my ability to develop a therapeutic relationship and actually be able to help clients deal with their issues and move on.

I learnt a lot more about interpersonal skills. I became a better listener. I learned how to be able to deal with a wide range of emotion and problems. In my opinion all the people I did meet and work with found counselling to be helpful and they gained a better understanding of themselves and were more capable of dealing with their issues and problems.

I don't really care about the mark now I am just happy to be a Ba. The only letters I thought I would have after my name were R.I.P.

I really enjoyed the graduation ceremony it felt much more like an achievement than my first one at college, the ceremony went on for about 2 hours and there were hundreds of people that graduated.

The annoying thing was turning up at the ceremony and going to collect my cap and gown and they had got my name wrong, there was no Tony Baker they had it down as Tom Baker. Thankfully it was corrected and my correct name was called out before I went on stage but I must've been the only person who graduated on that day and didn't come home with a degree.

I was really pleased that my father and his partner were there with me. Getting my degree was certainly the hardest thing I have ever done and the biggest achievement in my life and going on-stage and being acknowledged was certainly one of the proudest moments it was just a Shame my mother never got to see me graduate.

The one thing that I am sure of no matter what's around the corner Life Rolls On.

Figure 43;Tony Trevor Baker(B.A)